B. P. Pratten

The Scottish Anthem Book

For use in churches

B. P. Pratten

The Scottish Anthem Book
For use in churches

ISBN/EAN: 9783337240820

Printed in Europe, USA, Canada, Australia, Japan

Cover: Foto ©Lupo / pixelio.de

More available books at **www.hansebooks.com**

THE
Scottish Anthem Book

FOR USE IN CHURCHES

BY AUTHORITY OF THE GENERAL ASSEMBLY OF THE
CHURCH OF SCOTLAND

T. NELSON AND SONS
London, Edinburgh, and New York

1895

General Contents.

PREFACE, ...	iii
INDEX OF COMPOSERS, WITH THE NOS. OF THEIR ANTHEMS, ...	v
ALPHABETICAL INDEX,	vii
INDEX OF TEXTS,	x
INDEX OF TOPICS,	xiv
SECTION I.—CONTAINING, IN TEXTUAL ORDER, THE SIMPLER ANTHEMS, NOS. 1-82,	1
SECTION II.—CONTAINING, IN TEXTUAL ORDER, THE MORE ELABORATE ANTHEMS, NOS. 83-120,	193
SECTION III.—CONTAINING, IN TEXTUAL ORDER, WORDS OF ANTHEMS, NOS. 121-216,	409
INDEX OF WORDS OF ANTHEMS, NOS. 121-216,	423

Preface.

THIS Collection of Anthems is a revised and enlarged edition of the "Book of Anthems" published in 1875. Being intended primarily for use in the worship of the Church of Scotland, a short statement is desirable regarding the place of the Anthem in the Scottish Service.

Metrical Psalms, Prose Psalms, and Hymns are obviously best suited for congregational singing, and therefore should have the largest place in our praise; but a good Anthem gives useful variety to the service: it is one of those spiritual songs by which we may "speak to ourselves" or "teach and admonish one another."

Opinions differ as to whether the singing of the Anthem should in every case be left to the choir alone. A congregation may join silently in praise, as they do in prayer; and they may receive the teaching of the subject so interpreted for them by the choir, as they receive the teaching of the Scripture Lessons and Sermon; and the music of an Anthem is likely to be sung more expressively by a trained choir than by a mixed congregation. On the other hand, there are Anthems so simple that they may be joined in by the majority in a congregation of average musical culture; in such cases it would be inconsistent with the spirit and tradition of our Scottish Service to discourage them. A large number of pieces in this Collection are of this simple character; but in every case care has been taken that the music shall be devotionally expressive and intelligible.

The part of the service at which the Anthem may be introduced is left to the discretion of the minister, who is responsible for the order of service. It may be sung after one or other of the Scripture Lessons, or after the Sermon, or before the Benediction. but a Psalm or a Hymn, in which the whole congregation may join, is, as a rule, best suited for the closing act of praise. The minister should arrange that the Anthem be in tone or subject appropriate to the rest of the service. To facilitate selection of suitable Anthems, an Index of Topics has been provided.

The work is divided into three sections, and in each the Textual Anthems are placed first, in the order of the Books of the Bible; while the pieces with words from various sources, or with metrical words, follow. The Indexes and the Textual arrangement give ready reference to the whole contents of the book.

Section I. (Nos. 1-82) contains the simpler Anthems, and is published separately, forming a collection complete in itself, which some congregations may prefer. Section II. (Nos. 83-120) contains the more elaborate Anthems. Section III. (Nos. 121-216) contains words of Anthems approved by the Committee, but the music of which could not be printed owing to copyright restrictions. In the relative "Index of Words of Anthems," the composers, publishers, and sources of all the music for such words are given, that those who wish to use any of them may procure the sheets for themselves. In all the Indexes, Anthems which are given in words only are indicated by Italic type.

In a few of the smaller Anthems, a short Introduction has been written by the Musical Editor, with a view of establishing the key and indicating the *tempo* at which

PREFACE

these Anthems should be sung, much in the same way as in the playing over of Hymn tunes, etc. These preliminary bars are, of course, optional; they may be omitted, or others may be substituted by the organist.

The selection of Anthems has been made carefully by a special Sub-Committee of the Psalmody Committee of the Church of Scotland. In this they have had the able assistance of Mr. A. L. Peace, Mus. D., Organist of Glasgow Cathedral, and Musical Editor of this work; as well as of the "Scottish Hymnal" (1885), "The Book of Psalms and Paraphrases (in metre) with Tunes" (1886), and "The Psalter," being the Authorized Version of the Psalms, etc., pointed for Chanting, with accompanying Chants (1888): all prepared and published by authority of the Church of Scotland, for use in churches.

The Committee tender their thanks to the following composers and proprietors, for their generous permission, granted for the former edition, to print the copyright Anthems noted below :—

Rev. JOHN ALISON, D.D., for No. 63.
Rev. HENRY ALLON, D.D., for No. 82, from *Church Anthems.*
Mr. W. M. COOKE, M.D., for No. 7, from *Congregational Church Music.*
Mr. CHARLES DARNTON, for No. 12, from *Anthems for Church and Home.*
Sir GEORGE J. ELVEY, Mus. D., for No. 71.
The late Mr. J. S. GEIKIE, for No. 72.
The late Sir JOHN GOSS, Mus. D., for No. 6.
Mr. J. LOCKE GRAY, for No. 21, from his *Congregational Psalter.*
Mr. G. F. JACKMAN, for No. 13.
Sir HERBERT S. OAKELEY, Mus. D., for No. 102.
Rev. Dr. STEPHENSON, for his adaptation of words to No. 118.

The Committee also tender their acknowledgments to the following composers and proprietors whose copyrights have been inserted by arrangement, now or previously :—

Messrs. J. CURWEN AND SONS, for No. 28, from *Short Anthems for Choirs and Congregations.*
Mr. W. H. GILL, for Nos. 5, 55, 62.
The late Sir GEORGE A. MACFARREN, Mus. D., for No. 94.
Messrs. METZLER AND CO., for Nos. 4, 69, 98, 109, 111, from *The Choir;* and the words of Nos. 134, 172.
Messrs. W. MORLEY AND CO., for Nos. 90, 93, 100, from their series of *Original Anthems;* and for the words of No. 131.
Messrs. NOVELLO, EWER, AND CO., for Nos. 2, 3, 10, 14, 15, 16, 19, 29, 32, 33, 39, 49, 51, 78, 80, 87; and for the words of such Anthems in Section III. as are their copyright.
Mr. A. L. PEACE, Mus. D., for Nos. 11, 17, 24, 37, 54, 56, 60, 67, 85, 97, 99, 104, 106, 110, 115, 116, 119, 120; and for the symphonies and accompaniments which bear his initials.
Mr. JOHN SEWELL (Bridgnorth), for No. 105.
Mr. WILLIAM SPARK, Mus. D., for No. 83.
Mr. JOHN STEDMAN, for No. 53, from *Six Short Anthems for Cathedral and Parish Choirs.*
Mr. JOSEPH WILLIAMS, for No. 92.
Messrs. WEEKES AND CO., for No. 86.

The Committee express their great indebtedness to the Rev. John Alison, D.D., Edinburgh, for his services in connection with the whole of their musical publications, but more especially with the revision of the Psalter, and with this book. Special thanks are due to the Rev. James Rankin, D.D., Muthill, for preparing the Index of Topics; to the Rev. Alexander Galloway, B.D., Minto, for much valuable assistance; and to Mr. J. O. Anderson, Edinburgh, for preparing the Musical Indexes, and for constant and ungrudging care bestowed on the general arrangement and oversight of the work while passing through the press.

May 1891.

Alphabetical Index of Composers,

WITH THE NUMBERS OF THEIR ANTHEMS.

The List of Appointments stated in this Index as held by Composers is not meant to be exhaustive; usually the most important is given, or that held last. The best authorities have been consulted for the facts.
Anthems, the words only of which are given, are indicated by their Nos. being in Italic type.

COMPOSER OR SOURCE.	ANTHEM.
Abt, Franz Wilhelm, German Composer. 1819-1885.	*199.*
Allegri, Gregorio, Priest and Composer at the Cathedral of Fermo. 1580-1652.	73.
Allen, George Benjamin, Mus. B., Composer and Vocalist.	*169.*
Anonymous.	1, 76.
Attwood, Thomas, Organist of St. Paul's Cathedral. 1767-1838.	20, 34, 43, 70, 96, *211.*
Auber, Daniel-François-Esprit, French Composer. 1782-1871.	82.
Baker, Henry, Mus. B.	*162.*
Barnby, Joseph, Precentor and Organist of Eton College.	32, *145,* 190.
Bennett, Sir William Sterndale, M.A., D.C.L., Mus. D., Professor of Music in the University of Cambridge. 1816-1875.	188.
Best, William Thomas, Organist of St. George's Hall, Liverpool.	*150, 210.*
Bird, William, Organist of Chapel Royal. [1538]-1623.	147.
Boyce, William, Mus. D., Organist of the Chapel Royal. 1710-1779.	196.
Bradbury, William Batchelder, American Composer. 1816-1868.	22, 44.
Bridgewater, Thomas, Organist of St. Saviour's, York. Ob. 1831.	91.
Bühler, Franz Gregor, German Organist and Composer. 1760-1824.	120.
Calkin, John Baptiste, Professor at the Guildhall School of Music.	51, *131, 137.*
Callcott, John Wall, Mus. D., Lecturer at the Royal Institution. 1766-1821.	68.
Callcott, William Hutchins, son of preceding, Composer and Pianist. 1807-1882.	*141, 201.*
Camidge, John, Mus. D., Organist of York Cathedral. 1790-1859.	74.
Causton, Thomas, Organist and Composer. Ob. 1569.	81.
Cecil, Rev. Richard, Minister of St. John's Chapel, Bedford Row, London. 1748-1810.	58, 59.
Chipp, Edmund Thomas, Mus. D., Organist of Ely Cathedral. 1823-1886.	*191.*
Clarke-Whitfeld, John, Mus. D., Professor of Music in the University of Cambridge. 1770-1836.	30, 38, 88, 95, 101, *142, 144.*
Cooke, Benjamin, Mus. D., Organist of Westminster Abbey. 1734-1793.	108.
Costa, Sir Michael, Italian Composer and Conductor. 1810-1884.	92.
Couldrey, H. R., Organist of Holy Trinity Church, Windsor.	*175.*
Croft, William, Mus. D., Organist of Westminster Abbey. 1678-1727.	166.
Crotch, William, Mus. D., Professor of Music in the University of Oxford. 1775-1847.	27, 40.
Darnton, Charles, Organist of Park Chapel, Camden Town.	12.
Donizetti, Gaetano, Italian Composer. 1798-1848.	116.
Dykes, Rev. John Bacchus, M.A., Mus. D., Vicar of St. Oswald's, Durham. 1823-1876.	179, *204.*
Ebdon, Thomas, Organist of Durham Cathedral. 1738-1811.	112.
Elvey, Sir George Job, Organist of St. George's Chapel, Windsor (retired).	15, 28, 49, 71, *152, 155,* 156, 177, 185, 193, *212.*
Farrant, Richard, Organist of St. George's Chapel, Windsor. About 1530-1580. Also ascribed to John Hilton, Mus. B., Organist and Parish Clerk of St. Margaret's, Westminster. Ob. 1657.	65.
Gadsby, Henry Robert, Professor at the Guildhall School of Music.	*133.*
Garrett, George Mursell, M.A., Mus. D., Organist to the University of Cambridge.	*164,* 180.
Geikie, James Stewart, Choir Master in Augustine Church, Edinburgh. 1811-1883.	72.
Gibbons, Orlando, Mus. D., Organist of Westminster Abbey. 1583-1625.	75, *200.*
Gill, William Henry, Organist of Christ Church, Sidcup, Kent.	5, 55, 62.
Gladstone, Francis Edward, Mus. D., Organist and Composer.	100.
Goss, Sir John, Mus. D., Organist of St. Paul's Cathedral. 1800-1880.	6, 16, 78, *151, 153, 158,* 163, 165, 182, *184, 187,* 192, 194, *202, 203, 208.*
Gounod, Charles François, French Composer.	80, *134, 214.*
Greene, Maurice, Mus. D., Professor of Music in the University of Cambridge. 1695-1755.	23, *135.*
Handel, George Friedrich, Organist and Composer. 1685-1759.	41.

ALPHABETICAL INDEX OF COMPOSERS.

COMPOSER OR SOURCE.	ANTHEM.
Hatton, John Liptrot, Composer. 1809-1886	111, 172.
Hayes, Philip, Mus. D., Professor of Music in the University of Oxford. 1738-1797	8, 36.
Hewlett, Thomas, Mus. B., Organist of Newington Parish Church, Edinburgh. 1845-1874	63.
Hiles, Henry, Mus. D., Professor of Harmony at Owen's College, Manchester.	173.
Himmel, Friedrich Heinrich, Chapel Master to the King of Prussia. 1765-1814	14, 99.
Hopkins, Edward John, Mus. D., Organist of the Temple Church	183, 186, 207.
Hopkins, John Larkin, Mus. D., Organist of Trinity College, Cambridge. 1820-1873	2, 128, 138.
Jackman, George Frederick, Organist of the Parish Church, Hull (retired)	13.
Jackson, William, Organist of Exeter Cathedral. 1730-1803	77.
Jackson, William (Masham), Organist of Horton Chapel, Bradford. 1815-1866	50.
Kent, James, Organist of Winchester Cathedral. 1700-1776	84, 89.
King, Charles, Mus. B., Vicar Choral of St. Paul's Cathedral. 1687-1748	57.
Macfarren, Sir George Alexander, M.A., Mus. D., Professor of Music in the University of Cambridge. 1813-1887	4, 10, 94, 215.
Mackenzie, Alexander Campbell, Mus. D., Principal of the Royal Academy of Music.	124.
Malan, Rev. Cæsar Henri Abraham, D.D., Pastor at Geneva. 1787-1864	3.
Marchant, Arthur W., Mus. B., Organist of St. John's Parish Church, Sevenoaks, London	90, 93.
Mason, Lowell, Mus. D., American Composer. 1792-1872	31, 64.
Mendelssohn-Bartholdy, Felix, Ph. D., German Composer. 1809-1847	37, 107, 113, 126, 132, 139, 216.
Monk, William Henry, Mus. D., Professor of Vocal Music in King's College, London. 1823-1889	33.
Mozart, Johann Chrysostom Wolfgang Amadeus, Austrian Composer. 1756-1791	11, 79, 85, 103.
Nares, James, Mus. D., Organist of York Cathedral. 1715-1783	18, 25.
Naumann, Johann Gottlieb (or Giovanni Amadeo), Chapel Master to the Elector at Dresden. 1741-1801	67, 115.
Niedermeyer, Louis, Swiss Composer. 1802-1861	08.
Novello, Vincent, Organist, Composer, and Musical Editor. 1781-1861	19, 39, 129.
Oakeley, Sir Herbert Stanley, LL.D., Mus. D., Emeritus Professor of Music in the University of Edinburgh	102.
Ouseley, Rev. Sir Frederick Arthur Gore, Bart., M.A., LL.D., Mus. D., Professor of Music in the University of Oxford. 1825-1889	121, 130, 160, 167, 170.
Pattison, Thomas Moe, Organist of St. Mary's, Ealing	146, 148, 149.
Peace, Albert Lister, Mus. D., Organist of Glasgow Cathedral	24, 54, 56, 60, 97, 104, 106, 110, 119, 140, 174, 176, 205.
Prout, Ebenezer, Professor at the Royal Academy of Music	21.
Purcell, Henry, Organist of Westminster Abbey. 1658-1695	66.
Reynolds, John, Gentleman of Chapel Royal. Died 1770	9.
Richardson, Vaughan, Organist of Winchester Cathedral. Ob. 1729	26.
Rinck, Johann Christian Heinrich, Ph. D., Court Organist at Darmstadt. 1770-1846	52.
Roberts, John Varley, Mus. D., Organist of Magdalen College, Oxford	127.
Rossini, Gioacchino Antonio, Italian Composer. 1792-1868	209.
Russell, William, Mus. B., Organist of the Foundling Hospital. 1777-1813	118.
Scott, John, Organist at Spanish Town, Jamaica. 1776-1815	46.
Sewell, John, Organist at Bridgnorth	105.
Smart, Henry, Organist and Composer. 1813-1879	86, 109, 154, 206.
Smith, Robert Archibald, Precentor of St. George's Church, Edinburgh. 1780-1829	48.
Spark, William, Mus. D., Organist of Leeds Town Hall	83.
Spohr, Louis, German Composer and Violinist. 1784-1850	114, 117, 133, 198.
Stainer, Sir John, M.A., Mus. D., Professor of Music at the University of Oxford	169, 178, 181, 197.
Steggall, Charles, Mus. D., Organist of Lincoln's Inn	143.
Stewart, Sir Robert Prescott, Mus. D., Professor of Music in the University of Dublin	125, 189.
Sullivan, Sir Arthur Seymour, Mus. D., Composer and Conductor	87, 171.
Tallis, Thomas, Organist of Waltham Abbey. Ob. 1585	61.
Trimnell, Thomas Tallis, Mus. B., Organist in New Zealand	136, 168.
Tuckerman, Samuel Parkman, Mus. D., American Organist and Composer. 1819-1890	53.
Turle, James, Organist of Westminster Abbey. 1802-1882	157.
Tye, Christopher, Mus. D., Organist of Ely Cathedral. Ob. 1571 or 1572	35.
Webb, George James, Organist and Composer. 1803-1887	7.
Weldon, John, Organist of the Chapel Royal. About 1680-1736	45, 47.
Wesley, Samuel Sebastian, Mus. D., Organist of Gloucester Cathedral. 1810-1876	20, 69, 122, 195.
West, John Ebenezer, Organist and Composer	161.
Winter, Peter von, German Composer, 1754-1825	42.
Woodward, Rev. H. H., M.A., Mus. B., Minor Canon of Worcester Cathedral	213.
Zingarelli, Niccolo Antonio, Chapel Master of St. Peter's, Rome. 1752-1837	17.
Zionsharfe, Kocher's, 1855	76.

Alphabetical Index.

Anthems, the words only of which are given, are indicated by Italic type.

FIRST LINE.	COMPOSER OR SOURCE.	WORDS.	NO.
Abraham foresaw the gospel day	William Spark, Mus. D.	John viii. 56; Num. xxiv. 17; Isa. xxvi. 4	83
A day in thy courts	Sir George A. Macfarren, Mus. D.	Ps. lxxxiv. 10 12	91
Almighty and everlasting God	Orlando Gibbons, Mus. D.	Collect	200
Almighty and merciful God	Sir John Goss, Mus. D.	Collect	205
And every creature that is in heaven	Spohr	Rev. v. 13	114
Arise, shine; for thy light is come	Sir George J. Elvey, Mus. D.	Isa. lx. 1-3	49
As I live, saith the Lord	E. T. Chipp, Mus. D.	Rom. xiv. 11, 12; ii. 6, 11; viii. 14; xiv. 7, 8; xi. 33, 36	191
As pants the hart for cooling streams	Spohr. Arranged by James Stimpson	Ps. xlii. 1, 2 (Metrical)	133
Awake up, my glory	A. L. Peace, Mus. D.	Ps. lvii. 8-11	140
Behold, I bring you good tidings	W. H. Gill	Luke ii. 10, 11	55
Behold, I bring you good tidings	Sir John Goss, Mus. D.	Luke ii. 10, 11	182
Blessed are the merciful	Henry Hiles, Mus. D.	Matt. v. 7, 3, 8	173
Blessed are they that dwell in thy house	Arthur W. Marchant, Mus. B.	Ps. lxxxiv. 4, 5, 12	93
Blessed are they that fear the Lord	Sir George J. Elvey, Mus. D.	Ps. cxxviii. 1, 2	156
Blessed are they which are persecuted	A. L. Peace, Mus. D.	Matt. v. 10	174
Blessed be the God and Father	S. S. Wesley, Mus. D.	1 Pet. i. 3-5, 15, 17, 22-25	195
Blessed be the Lord God, even the God of Israel	James Nares, Mus. D	Ps. lxxii. 18, 19	25
Blessed be the Lord God of Israel	A. L. Peace, Mus. D.	Luke i. 68-79	110
Blessed be the Lord God of Israel	Rev. J. B. Dykes, Mus. D.	Luke i. 68-79	179
Blessed be the Lord God of Israel	G. M. Garrett, M.A., Mus. D.	Luke i. 68-79	180
Blessed be the Lord God of Israel	Sir John Stainer, M.A., Mus. D.	Luke i. 68-79	181
Blessed be thou, Lord God of Israel	James Kent	1 Chron. xxix. 10-13	64
Blessed is he that considereth the poor	James Nares, Mus. D.	Ps. xli. 1	18
Blessed is the man that feareth the Lord	J. Clarke-Whitfeld, Mus. D.	Ps. cxii. 1-3	101
Blessing, and glory, and wisdom	William Boyce, Mus. D.	Rev. vii. 12	196
Blessing, honour, glory, and power	Spohr	Rev. v. 13	114
Blest are the departed	Spohr	Rev. xiv. 13	198
Bow thine ear, O Lord, and hear	William Bird	Ps. lxxxvi. 1; Isa. lxiv. 10	147
By the waters of Babylon	George B. Allen, Mus. B.	Ps. cxxxvii.	150
Call to remembrance, O Lord	Charles Darnton	Ps. xxv. 6, 7	12
Call to remembrance thy tender mercies	Vincent Novello	Ps. xxv. 6; vi. 4	120
Cast thy burden on the Lord	W. B. Bradbury	Ps. lv. 22	22
Christ being raised from the dead	W. H. Gill	Rom. vi. 9-11	62
Christ is risen from the dead	Sir George J. Elvey, Mus. D.	1 Cor. xv. 20; Rom. vi. 10	193
Christ our passover is sacrificed for us	Sir John Goss, Mus. D.	1 Cor. v. 7, 8	192
Come, and let us go up	A. L. Peace, Mus. D.	Micah iv. 2-4	106
Come, and let us return unto the Lord	William Jackson (Masham)	Hosea vi. 1; Isa. lv. 7	50
Come, Holy Ghost, our souls inspire	Thomas Attwood	Tr. Cosin's Devotions, 1627	211
Come, Holy Ghost, our souls inspire	Sir George J. Elvey, Mus. D.	Tr. Cosin's Devotions, 1627	212
Come unto me, all ye that labour	S. P. Tuckerman, Mus. D	Matt. xi. 28, 29	53
Come unto me, all ye that labour	H. R. Couldrey	Matt. xi. 28, 29	175
Comfort, O Lord, the soul of thy servant	William Crotch, Mus. D.	Ps. lxxxvi. 4	27
Create in me a clean heart, O God	Ebenezer Prout, B.A.	Ps. li. 10-13	21
Cry aloud, and shout	William Croft, Mus. D.	Isa. xii. 6	106
Daughters of Jerusalem	Sir George J. Elvey, Mus. D.	Luke xxiii. 28	185
Enter not into judgment with thy servant	Thomas Attwood	Ps. cxliii. 2	43
From the rising of the sun	Sir F. A. Gore Ouseley, Bart., Mus. D.	Mal. i. 11	170
From thy love as a Father	Charles Gounod	Hymn	214
Give ear, O Lord, unto my prayer	T. Mee Pattison	Ps. lxxxvi. 6, 7	148
Give peace in our time, O Lord	W. Hutchins Callcott	Liturgy	201
God be merciful unto us, and bless us	A. L. Peace, Mus. D.	Ps. lxvii.	24
God be merciful unto us, and bless us	Thomas Bridgewater	Ps. lxvii.	91
God is a Spirit	Sir W. Sterndale Bennett, Mus. D.	John iv. 24, 23	188
God is our hope and strength	Maurice Greene, Mus. D.	Ps. xlvi. 1-3, 5, 8-10	135
God so loved the world	Sir John Goss, Mus. D.	John iii. 16, 17	187
Grant us thy peace, Almighty Lord	Mendelssohn	Hymn	216
Grant, we beseech thee, merciful Lord	John Wall Callcott, Mus. D.	Collect	68
Hallelujah! What are these that are arrayed?	Sir John Stainer, M.A., Mus. D.	Rev. vii. 13-17	197

ALPHABETICAL INDEX.

FIRST LINE.	COMPOSER OR SOURCE.	WORDS.	NO.
Hear me when I call	Sir George A. Macfarren, Mus. D.	Ps. iv. 1, 6, 8	4
Hear my prayer, O God; and hide not	James Kent	Ps. lv. 1, 2, 4, 5	89
Hear my prayer, O God, incline thine ear	Mendelssohn	Ps. lv. 1-7 (Metrical)	139
Hear my prayer, O Lord, and give ear	Nicolo Zingarelli. Adapted to English words by A. L. Peace, Mus. D.	Ps. xxxix. 12, 13; xxxv. 9	17
Hear my prayer, O Lord; give ear	Peter von Winter. Adapted to English words by William Shore	Ps. cxliii. 1	42
Hear, O Lord, and have mercy upon me	Sir F. A. Gore Ouseley, Bart., Mus. D.	Ps. xxx. 10-12	130
Hear, O thou Shepherd of Israel	J. Clarke-Whitfeld, Mus. D.	Ps. lxxx. 1, 3-5, 8, 10-12, 14, 18	144
Hear the voice and prayer of thy servants	J. L. Hopkins, Mus. D.	1 Kings viii. 28-30	2
He that shall endure to the end	Mendelssohn	Matt. xxiv. 13	107
Holy, holy, holy: holy art thou	William Russell, Mus. B.	Sanctus and Hosanna	118
Holy, holy, holy is God our Lord	Spohr	Sanctus	117
Holy, holy, holy Lord God of hosts	Thomas Attwood	Sanctus	70
Holy, holy, holy Lord God of hosts	Sir George J. Elvey, Mus. D.	Sanctus	71
Holy, holy, holy Lord God of hosts	G. B. Allegri	Sanctus	73
Holy, holy, holy Lord God of hosts	John Camidge, Mus. D.	Sanctus	74
Holy, holy, holy Lord God of hosts	Orlando Gibbons, Mus. D	Sanctus	75
Holy, holy, holy Lord God of sabaoth	James S. Geikie	Sanctus	72
Holy, holy: thou, O Lord, alone art holy	From a Sanctus in Kocher's Zionsharfe, 1855	Sanctus	76
Honour and glory, dominion, power	Johann Christian Heinrich Rinck	Various texts	52
How beautiful upon the mountains	R. A. Smith	Isa. lii. 7, 9	48
How dear are thy counsels unto me, O God	William Crotch, Mus. D.	Ps. cxxxix. 17, 23, 24	40
How goodly are thy tents, O Jacob	Sir F. A. Gore Ouseley, Bart., Mus. D.	Num. xxiv. 5, 6	121
How lovely are the messengers	Mendelssohn	2 Cor. v. 20; Rom. x. 15, 18	113
I believe in God the Father Almighty	E. J. Hopkins, Mus. D.	Apostles' Creed	207
I believe in one God, the Father Almighty	Sir John Goss, Mus. D.	Nicene Creed	208
If we believe that Jesus died	Sir John Goss, Mus. D.	1 Thess. iv. 14, 18	194
If ye love me, keep my commandments	Thomas Tallis	John xiv. 15-17	61
If ye love me, keep my commandments	Sir Robert P. Stewart, Mus. D.	John xiv. 15-17, 27	189
Incline thine ear to me	F. H. Himmel. Adapted to English words by William Patten	Ps. xxxi. 2, 10	14
In Jewry is God known	J. Clarke-Whitfeld, Mus. D.	Ps. lxxvi. 1-3	142
In the Lord put I my trust	Sir Robert P. Stewart, Mus. D.	Ps. xi. 1, 2, 4, 6, 7	125
I shall see him, but not now	William Spark, Mus. D.	John viii. 56; Num. xxiv. 17; Isa. xxvi. 4	83
It is a good thing to give thanks	T. Mee Pattison	Ps. xcii. 1-4	149
It is high time to awake out of sleep	Joseph Barnby	Rom. xiii. 11, 12	190
I waited for the Lord	Mendelssohn	Ps. xl. 1, 4	132
I was glad when they said unto me	Sir George J. Elvey, Mus. D.	Ps. cxxii. 1, 5-7	155
I will alway give thanks	J. Clarke-Whitfeld, Mus. D.	Ps. xxxiv. 1-3	88
I will arise, and go to my Father	Rev. Richard Cecil	Luke xv. 18, 19	58
I will arise, and go to my Father	Rev. Richard Cecil. Harmonized and arranged by William Jackson	Luke xv. 18, 19	50
I will cry unto God with my voice	Charles Steggall, Mus. D.	Ps. lxxvii. 1, 3, 5, 6, 11, 12	143
I will extol thee, my God, O King	W. B. Bradbury	Ps. cxlv. 1-3	44
I will lay me down in peace	W. H. Gill	Ps. iv. 8	5
I will lay me down in peace	Henry Gadsby	Ps. iv. 8	123
I will lay me down in peace	A. C. Mackenzie, Mus. D.	Ps. iv. 8	124
I will lift up mine eyes unto the hills	J. Clarke-Whitfeld, Mus. D.	Ps. cxxi. 1, 2, 5-8	38
I will magnify thee, O God, my King	Sir John Goss, Mus. D.	Ps. cxlv. 1, 2, 15, 16	163
I will sing of the Lord	Mozart. Adapted to English words by A. L. Peace, Mus. D.	Ps. xiii. 6	85
I will wash my hands in innocence	G. F. Jackman	Ps. xxvi. 6	13
Jesus, Lord, thou Son eternal	Mozart	Ave verum	79
Jesu, Word of God incarnate	Charles Gounod	Ave verum	80
Keep innocency, and take heed	J. Baptiste Calkin	Ps. xxxvii. 37-40	131
Lamb of God, that takest away	J. G. Naumann. Adapted to English words by A. L. Peace, Mus. D.	Agnus Dei	67
Let the people praise thee, O God	Sir Michael Costa	Ps. lxvii. 5, 6, 1	92
Let us now fear the Lord our God	John Sewell (Bridgnorth)	Jer. v. 24; xxxiii. 11	105
Let us now go even unto Bethlehem	J. L. Hatton	Luke ii. 15, 10, 11	111
Let us now go even unto Bethlehem	E. J. Hopkins, Mus. D.	Luke ii. 15, 10, 11	183
Lift up your heads, O ye gates	J. L. Hopkins, Mus. D.	Ps. xxiv. 7, 8, 10	128
Like as the hart desireth the water brooks	Vincent Novello. Adapted to English words by R. R. Ross	Ps. xlii. 1, 5	19
Lord, for thy tender mercies' sake	Richard Farrant. Also ascribed to John Hilton, Mus. B.	From Lydley's Prayers	65
Lord, have mercy upon us	J. G. Naumann. Adapted to English words by A. L. Peace, Mus. D.	Agnus Dei	115

ALPHABETICAL INDEX. ix

FIRST LINE.	COMPOSER OR SOURCE.	WORDS	NO.
Lord, hear my prayer	Louis Niedermeyer	Ps. cii. 1; vi. 4	98
Lord, how long wilt thou forget me?	Mendelssohn	Ps. xiii. 1, 2	126
Lord, I call upon thee	Sir F. A. Gore Ouseley, Bart., Mus. D.	Ps. cxli. 1, 2	109
Lord, I call upon thee	John E. West	Ps. cxli. 1, 2	161
Lord, now lettest thou thy servant	A. L. Peace, Mus. D.	Luke ii. 29-32	56
Lord, now lettest thou thy servant	Charles King, Mus. B.	Luke ii. 29-32	57
Lord, now lettest thou thy servant	Thomas Ebdon	Luke ii. 29-32	112
Lord, now lettest thou thy servant	Sir John Goss, Mus. D.	Luke ii. 29-32	185
Lord of all power and might	S. S. Wesley, Mus. D.	Collect	130
Lord, who shall dwell in thy tabernacle?	J. Varley Roberts, Mus. D.	Ps. xv. 1-5	127
Mine eyes look unto thee, O Lord God	Henry Baker, Mus. B.	Ps. cxli. 8	162
My God, look upon me	John Reynolds	Ps. xxii. 1-3	9
My song shall be of mercy and judgment	Lowell Mason, Mus. D.	Ps. ci. 1, 2	31
My soul doth magnify the Lord	A. L. Peace, Mus. D.	Luke i. 46-55	54
My soul doth magnify the Lord	Benjamin Cooke, Mus. D.	Luke i. 46-55	108
My soul doth magnify the Lord	Henry Smart	Luke i. 46-55	109
My soul doth magnify the Lord	A. L. Peace, Mus. D.	Luke i. 46-55	176
My soul doth magnify the Lord	Sir George J. Elvey, Mus. D.	Luke i. 46-55	177
My soul doth magnify the Lord	Sir John Stainer, M.A., Mus. D.	Luke i. 46-55	178
My soul truly waiteth still upon God	Arthur W. Marchant, Mus. B.	Ps. lxii. 1, 6, 8	90
My voice shalt thou hear in the morning	Sir John Goss, Mus. D.	Ps. v. 3, 7	6
Now unto him that is able to keep us from falling	Lowell Mason, Mus. D.	Jude 24, 25	64
Now we are ambassadors in the name	Mendelssohn	2 Cor. v. 20; Rom. x. 15, 18	113
Now when Jesus was born in Bethlehem	J. L. Hatton	Matt. ii. 1, 2; Luke i. 32, 33	172
O be joyful in the Lord, all ye lands	S. S. Wesley, Mus. D.	Ps. c.	29
O be joyful in the Lord, all ye lands	J. Clarke-Whitfeld, Mus. D.	Ps. c.	30
O be joyful in the Lord, all ye lands	A. L. Peace, Mus. D.	Ps. c.	97
O be joyful in the Lord, all ye lands	Sir John Goss, Mus. D.	Ps. c.	151
O clap your hands together	T. Tallis Trimnell, Mus. B.	Ps. xlvii. 1, 2	136
O give thanks unto the Lord, and call	Sir George J. Elvey, Mus. D.	Ps. cv. 1-3	152
O give thanks unto the Lord; for he	Sir John Goss, Mus. D.	Ps. cvi. 1, 2; cxviii. 22, 23, 29	153
O God, thou art worthy to be praised	Sir Arthur S. Sullivan, Mus. D.	Tobit viii. 15-17; Ps. xx. 2, 4, 1	171
O Holy Ghost, into our minds	Sir George A. Macfarren, Mus. D.	Hymn	215
O how amiable are thy dwellings	Vaughan Richardson	Ps. lxxxiv. 1, 2, 4	26
O how amiable are thy dwellings	Joseph Barnby	Ps. lxxxiv. 1, 2, 4	145
O how amiable are thy dwellings	T. Mee Pattison	Ps. lxxxiv. 1-5	146
O Lord God of my salvation	J. Clarke-Whitfeld, Mus. D.	Ps. lxxxviii. 1-3, 7; lxxxvi. 15, 16	95
O Lord, how manifold are thy works	Joseph Barnby	Ps. civ. 24; lxv. 13; ciii. 2	32
O Lord, in thee is all my trust	Thomas Causton	Psalm (Metrical)	81
O Lord most holy, O God most mighty	Franz Abt	Ave Maria	199
O Lord my God, hear thou the prayer	Rev. H. A. Cæsar Malan, D.D.	1 Kings viii. 28, 30	3
O Lord my God, hear thou the prayer	S. S. Wesley, Mus. D.	1 Kings viii. 28, 30	122
O Lord my strength, to thee I pray	Auber	O Salutaris	82
O Lord, thou art my God	Sir F. A. Gore Ouseley, Bart., Mus. D.	Isa. xxv. 1	167
O Lord, thy word endureth	Christopher Tye, Mus. D.	Ps. cxix. 89-91	35
O Lord, we pray thee	Donizetti. Adapted to English words by A. L. Peace, Mus. D.	Ave Maria	116
O Lord, we trust alone in thee	Handel	Ps. cxli. 8	41
O love the Lord, all ye his saints	Sir Arthur S. Sullivan, Mus. D.	Ps. xxxi. 26, 27	87
O praise God in his holiness	John Weldon	Ps. cl. 1-4, 6	47
O praise the Lord, all ye nations	Sir Herbert S. Oakeley, Mus. D.	Ps. cxvii.	102
O praise the Lord, for it is a good thing	John Weldon	Ps. cxlvii. 1, 5	45
O praise the Lord. Laud ye the name	Sir John Goss, Mus. D.	Ps. cxxxv. 1-3, 19, 20	158
O Saviour of the world	Sir John Goss, Mus. D.	Collect	202
O taste and see how gracious the Lord is	Sir John Goss, Mus. D.	Ps. xxxiv. 8-10	16
Out of the deep have I called unto thee	Mozart	Ps. cxxx. 1-4	103
O worship the Lord in the beauty of holiness	Sir George J. Elvey, Mus. D.	Ps. xcvi. 9; lxviii. 4	23
Praise the Lord, O Jerusalem	John Scott	Ps. cxlvii. 12; cxlviii. 2, 3; cvii. 8	46
Praise the Lord, O my soul	Sir John Goss, Mus. D.	Ps. cxlvi. 1, 2; cxlvi. 6-9; cxxv. 1, 2	165
Pray for the peace of Jerusalem	Vincent Novello	Ps. cxxii. 6, 7	39
Rejoice in the Lord, O ye righteous	Sir George J. Elvey, Mus. D.	Ps. xxxiii. 1, 2	15
Rend your heart, and not your garments	J. Baptiste Calkin	Joel ii. 13	51
Righteous art thou, O Lord	Philip Hayes, Mus. D.	Ps. cxix. 137, 142, 143	36
Righteous art thou, O Lord	Mendelssohn. Adapted to English words by A. L. Peace, Mus. D.	Ps. cxix. 137, 33, 114, 117, 171	37
Save me, O God, for thy name's sake	J. L. Hopkins, Mus. D.	Ps. liv. 1, 3	138
Send out thy light and thy truth	Charles Gounod	Ps. xliii. 3-5; xx. 6-8	134
Suffer little children to come unto me	A. L. Peace, Mus. D.	Luke xviii. 16, 17	60

INDEX OF TEXTS

FIRST LINE.	COMPOSER OR SOURCE.	WORDS.	NO.
Teach me, O Lord, the way of thy statutes	Thomas Attwood	Ps. cxix. 33	34
The Lord bless thee, and keep thee	Anonymous. Harmony by Lowell Mason, Mus. D.	Num. vi. 24-26	1
The Lord descended from above	Philip Hayes, Mus. D.	Ps. xviii. 9, 10 (Metrical)	8
The Lord is full of compassion	F. H. Himmel. Adapted to English words by A. L. Peace, Mus. D.	Ps. ciii. 8, 9	99
The Lord is full of compassion	F. E. Gladstone, Mus. D.	Ps. ciii. 8, 10-13	100
The Lord is great in Zion	W. T. Best	Ps. xcix. 2, 5, 9	150
The Lord is loving unto every man	G. M. Garrett, M.A., Mus. D.	Ps. cxlv. 9-13	164
The Lord is my shepherd	Sir George A. Macfarren, Mus. D.	Ps. xxiii. 1-4, 6	10
The Lord is my shepherd	Henry Smart	Ps. xxiii.	86
The Lord is my strength and my song	W. H. Monk, Mus. D.	Ps. cxviii. 14, 19, 22, 24	33
The Lord is my strength and my song	Henry Smart	Ps. cxviii. 14, 17, 29	154
The Lord that made heaven and earth	James Turle	Ps. cxxxiv. 3	157
The Lord will be a refuge for the oppressed	From G. J. Webb	Ps. ix. 9, 10	7
The night is far spent	Thomas Hewlett, Mus. B.	Rom. xiii. 12	63
The radiant morn hath passed away	Rev. H. H. Woodward, M.A., Mus. B.	Hymn	213
The sacrifices of God are a broken spirit	J. Baptiste Calkin	Ps. li. 17	137
The sun shall be no more thy light by day	A. L. Peace, Mus. D.	Isa. lx. 19, 20	104
Thine, O Lord, is the greatness	James Kent	1 Chron. xxix. 10-13	84
Thy memory, O Jesus sweet	Franz G. Bühler. Adapted to English words by A. L. Peace, Mus. D.	Jesu dulcis memoria	120
Thou knowest, Lord, the secrets of our hearts	Henry Purcell	Burial Service	66
Thou visitest the earth, and blessest it	Maurice Greene, Mus. D.	Ps. lxv. 9, 11	23
Thou visitest the earth, and blessest it	W. Hutchins Callcott	Ps. lxv. 9, 11, 13	141
Thou wilt keep him in perfect peace	T. Tallis Trimnell, Mus. B.	Isa. xxvi. 3	168
To thee, great Lord o'er all	Rossini	Ps. cxxxvii. 1-4 (Metrical)	209
Turn thee again, O Lord, at the last	Thomas Attwood	Ps. xc. 13	96
Turn thy face from my sins	Thomas Attwood	Ps. li. 9-11	20
Unto thee, O Lord, do I lift up my soul	Mozart. Adapted to English words by A. L. Peace, Mus. D.	Ps. xxv. 1, 2; ix. 1, 2	11
We praise thee, O God	William Jackson (Exeter)	Te Deum laudamus	77
We praise thee, O God	Sir John Goss, Mus. D.	Te Deum laudamus	78
We praise thee, O God	A. L. Peace, Mus. D.	Te Deum laudamus	119
We praise thee, O God	Rev. J. B. Dykes, Mus. D.	Te Deum laudamus	204
We praise thee, O God	A. L. Peace, Mus. D.	Te Deum laudamus	205
We praise thee, O God	Henry Smart	Te Deum laudamus	206
What are these that are arrayed?	Sir John Stainer, M.A., Mus. D.	Rev. vii. 13-17	197
While shepherds watched their flocks by night	W. T. Best	Luke ii. 8-15 (Metrical)	210
Why seek ye the living among the dead?	E. J. Hopkins, Mus. D.	Luke xxiv. 5-7	186
Ye shall dwell in the land that I gave	Sir John Stainer, M.A., Mus. D.	Ezek. xxxvi. 28, 30, 31, 35; Ps. cxxxvi. 1; and Hymn	169

Index of Texts.

Anthems, the words only of which are given, are indicated by Italic type.

WORDS FROM THE OLD TESTAMENT.

WORDS.	FIRST LINE.	COMPOSER OR SOURCE.	NO.
Num. vi. 24-26	The Lord bless thee, and keep thee	Anonymous. Harmony by Lowell Mason, Mus. D.	1
" xxiv. 5, 6	*How goodly are thy tents, O Jacob*	Sir F. A. Gore Ouseley, Bart., Mus. D.	121
" xxiv. 17; Isa. xxvi. 4.	I shall see him, but not now	William Spark, Mus. D.	83
1 Kings viii. 28-30	Hear the voice and prayer of thy servants	J. L. Hopkins, Mus. D.	2
" viii. 28, 30	O Lord my God, hear thou the prayer	Rev. H. A. Cæsar Malan, D.D.	3
" viii. 28, 30	O Lord my God, hear thou the prayer	S. S. Wesley, Mus. D.	122
1 Chron. xxix. 10-13	Blessed be thou, Lord God of Israel; Thine, O Lord, is the greatness	James Kent	84
Ps. iv. 1, 6, 8	Hear me when I call	Sir George A. Macfarren, Mus. D.	4
" iv. 8	I will lay me down in peace	W. H. Gill	5
" iv. 8	I will lay me down in peace	Henry Gadsby	123
" iv. 8	I will lay me down in peace	A. C. Mackenzie, Mus. D.	124
" v. 3, 7	My voice shalt thou hear in the morning	Sir John Goss, Mus. D.	6
" ix. 9, 10	The Lord will be a refuge for the oppressed	From G. J. Webb	7

INDEX OF TEXTS.

WORDS.	FIRST LINE.	COMPOSER OR SOURCE.	NO.
Ps. xi. 1, 2, 4, 6, 7	In the Lord put I my trust	Sir Robert P. Stewart, Mus. D.	125
" xiii. 6	I will sing of the Lord	Mozart. Adapted to English words by A. L. Peace, Mus. D.	55
" xiii. 1, 2	Lord, how long wilt thou forget me?	Mendelssohn	1.6
" xv. 1-5	Lord, who shall dwell in thy tabernacle?	J. Varley Roberts, Mus. D.	127
" xviii. 9, 10 (Metrical)	The Lord descended from above	Philip Hayes, Mus. D.	8
" xxii. 1-3	My God, look upon me	John Reynolds	9
" xxiii. 1-4, 6	The Lord is my shepherd	Sir George A. Macfarren, Mus. D.	10
" xxiii.	The Lord is my shepherd	Henry Smart	86
" xxiv. 7, 8, 10	Lift up your heads, O ye gates	J. L. Hopkins, Mus. D.	128
" xxv. 1, 2; ix. 1, 2	Unto thee, O Lord, do I lift up my soul	Mozart. Adapted to English words by A. L. Peace, Mus. D.	11
" xxv. 6, 7	Call to remembrance, O Lord	Charles Darnton	12
" xxv. 6; vi. 4	Call to remembrance thy tender mercies	Vincent Novello	129
" xxvi. 6	I will wash my hands in innocency	G. F. Jackman	13
" xxx. 10-12	Hear, O Lord, and have mercy upon me	Sir F. A. Gore Ouseley, Bart., Mus. D.	130
" xxxi. 2, 16	Incline thine ear to me	F. H. Himmel. Adapted to English words by William Patten.	14
" xxxi. 26, 27	O love the Lord, all ye his saints	Sir Arthur S. Sullivan, Mus. D.	87
" xxxiii. 1, 2	Rejoice in the Lord, O ye righteous	Sir George J. Elvey, Mus. D.	15
" xxxiv. 1-3	I will alway give thanks	J. Clarke-Whitfeld, Mus. D.	88
" xxxiv. 8-10	O taste and see how gracious the Lord is	Sir John Goss, Mus. D.	16
" xxxvii. 37, 40	Keep innocency, and take heed	J. Baptiste Calkin	131
" xxxix. 12, 13; xxxv. 9	Hear my prayer, O Lord, and give ear	Nicolo Zingarelli. Adapted to English words by A. L. Peace, Mus. D.	17
" xl. 1, 4	I waited for the Lord	Mendelssohn	132
" xli. 1	Blessed is he that considereth the poor	James Nares, Mus. D.	18
" xlii. 1, 2 (Metrical)	As pants the hart for cooling streams	Spohr. Arranged by James Stimpson	133
" xlii. 1, 5	Like as the hart desireth the water brooks	Vincent Novello. Adapted to English words by R. R. Ross.	19
" xliii. 3-5; xx. 6-8	Send out thy light and thy truth	Charles Gounod	134
" xlvi. 1-3, 5, 8-10	God is our hope and strength	Maurice Greene, Mus. D.	135
" xlvii. 1, 2	O clap your hands together	T. Tallis Trimnell, Mus. D.	136
" li. 9-11	Turn thy face from my sins	Thomas Attwood	20
" li. 10-13	Create in me a clean heart, O God	Ebenezer Prout, B.A.	21
" li. 17	The sacrifices of God are a broken spirit	J. Baptiste Calkin	137
" liv. 1, 3	Save me, O God, for thy name's sake	J. L. Hopkins, Mus. D.	138
" lv. 1, 2, 4, 5	Hear my prayer, O God; and hide not	James Kent	80
" lv. 1-7 (Metrical)	Hear my prayer, O God, incline thine ear	Mendelssohn	139
" lv. 22	Cast thy burden on the Lord	W. B. Bradbury	22
" lvii. 8-11	Awake up, my glory	A. L. Peace, Mus. D.	140
" lxii. 1, 6, 8	My soul truly waiteth still upon God	Arthur W. Marchant, Mus. B.	90
" lxv. 9, 11	Thou visitest the earth, and blessest it	Maurice Greene, Mus. D.	23
" lxv. 9, 11, 13	Thou visitest the earth, and blessest it	W. Hutchins Callcott	141
" lxvii.	God be merciful unto us, and bless us	A. L. Peace, Mus. D.	24
" lxvii.	God be merciful unto us, and bless us	Thomas Bridgewater	91
" lxvii. 5, 6, 1	Let the people praise thee, O God	Sir Michael Costa	92
" lxxii. 18, 19	Blessed be the Lord God, even the God of Israel	James Nares, Mus. D.	25
" lxxvi. 1-3	In Jewry is God known	J. Clarke-Whitfeld, Mus. D.	142
" lxxvii. 1, 3, 5, 6, 11, 12	I will cry unto God with my voice	Charles Steggall, Mus. D.	143
" lxxx. 1, 3-5, 8, 10-12, 14, 18	Hear, O thou Shepherd of Israel	J. Clarke-Whitfeld, Mus. D.	144
" lxxxiv. 1, 2, 4	O how amiable are thy dwellings	Vaughan Richardson	26
" lxxxiv. 1, 2, 4	O how amiable are thy dwellings	Joseph Barnby	145
" lxxxiv. 1-5	O how amiable are thy dwellings	T. Mee Pattison	146
" lxxxiv. 4, 5, 12	Blessed are they that dwell in thy house	Arthur W. Marchant, Mus. B.	93
" lxxxiv. 10-12	A day in thy courts	Sir George A. Macfarren, Mus. D.	94
" lxxxvi. 4	Comfort, O Lord, the soul of thy servant	William Crotch, Mus. D.	27
" lxxxvi. 1; Isa. lxiv. 10	Bow thine ear, O Lord, and hear	William Bird	147
" lxxxvi. 1	Give ear, O Lord, unto my prayer	T. Mee Pattison	148
" lxxxviii.1-3, 7; lxxxvi. 15, 16	O Lord God of my salvation	J. Clarke-Whitfeld, Mus. D.	95
" xc. 13	Turn thee again, O Lord, at the last	Thomas Attwood	96
" xcii. 1-4	It is a good thing to give thanks	T. Mee Pattison	149
" xcvi. 9; lxviii. 4	O worship the Lord in the beauty of holiness	Sir George J. Elvey, Mus. D.	28
" xcix. 2, 5, 9	The Lord is great in Zion	W. T. Best	150
" c.	O be joyful in the Lord, all ye lands	S. S. Wesley, Mus. D.	29
" c.	O be joyful in the Lord, all ye lands	J. Clarke-Whitfeld, Mus. D.	30
" c.	O be joyful in the Lord, all ye lands	A. L. Peace, Mus. D.	97
" c.	O be joyful in the Lord, all ye lands	Sir John Goss, Mus. D.	151
" ci. 1, 2	My song shall be of mercy and judgment	Lowell Mason, Mus. D.	31
" cii. 1; vi. 4	Lord, hear my prayer	Louis Niedermeyer	98

INDEX OF TEXTS.

WORDS.	FIRST LINE.	COMPOSER OR SOURCE.	NO.
Ps. ciii. 8, 9	The Lord is full of compassion	F. H. Himmel. Adapted to English words by A. L. Peace, Mus. D.	99
" ciii. 8, 10–13	The Lord is full of compassion	F. E. Gladstone, Mus. D.	100
" civ. 24 ; lxv. 13 ; ciii. 2.	O Lord, how manifold are thy works	Joseph Darnby	lxx
" cv. 1–3	O give thanks unto the Lord, and call	Sir George J. Elvey, Mus. D.	152
" cvi. 1, 2 ; cxviii. 22, 23, 29.	O give thanks unto the Lord ; for he	Sir John Goss, Mus. D.	153
" cxii. 1–3	Blessed is the man that feareth the Lord	J. Clarke-Whitfeld, Mus. D.	101
" cxvii.	O praise the Lord, all ye nations	Sir Herbert S. Oakeley, Mus. D.	102
" cxviii. 14, 19, 22, 24	The Lord is my strength and my song	W. H. Monk, Mus. D.	33
" cxviii. 14, 17, 29	The Lord is my strength and my song	Henry Smart	154
" cxix. 33	Teach me, O Lord, the way of thy statutes	Thomas Attwood	34
" cxix. 89–91	O Lord, thy word endureth	Christopher Tye, Mus. D.	35
" cxix. 137, 142, 143	Righteous art thou, O Lord	Philip Hayes, Mus. D.	36
" cxix.137, 33, 114, 117, 171.	Righteous art thou, O Lord	Mendelssohn. Adapted to English words by A. L. Peace, Mus. D.	37
" cxxi. 1, 2, 5–8	I will lift up mine eyes unto the hills	J. Clarke-Whitfeld, Mus. D.	38
" cxxii. 1, 5–7	I was glad when they said unto me	Sir George J. Elvey, Mus. D.	155
" cxxii. 6, 7	Pray for the peace of Jerusalem	Vincent Novello	39
" cxxviii. 1, 2	Blessed are they that fear the Lord	Sir George J. Elvey, Mus. D.	156
" cxxx. 1–4	Out of the deep have I called unto thee	Mozart	103
" cxxxiv. 3	The Lord that made heaven and earth	James Turle	157
" cxxxv. 1–3, 19, 20	O praise the Lord. Laud ye the name	Sir John Goss, Mus. D.	158
" cxxxvii. 1–4 (Metrical)	To thee, great Lord o'er all	Rossini	200
" cxxxvii.	By the waters of Babylon	George B. Allen, Mus. B.	159
" cxxxix. 17, 23, 24	How dear are thy counsels unto me, O God	William Crotch, Mus. D.	40
" cxli. 1, 2	Lord, I call upon thee	Sir F. A. Gore Ouseley, Bart., Mus. D.	160
" cxli. 1, 2	Lord, I call upon thee	John E. West	161
" cxli. 8	O Lord, we trust alone in thee	Handel	41
" cxli. 8	Mine eyes look unto thee, O Lord God	Henry Baker, Mus. B.	162
" cxliii. 1	Hear my prayer, O Lord ; give ear	Peter von Winter. Adapted to English words by William Shore	42
" cxliii. 2	Enter not into judgment with thy servant	Thomas Attwood	43
" cxlv. 1–3	I will extol thee, my God, O King	W. B. Bradbury	44
" cxlv. 1, 2, 15, 16	I will magnify thee, O God, my King	Sir John Goss, Mus. D.	163
" cxlv. 9–13	The Lord is loving unto every man	G. M. Garrett, M.A., Mus. D.	164
" cxlvi. 1, 2 ; cxxii. 6–9 ; cxxv. 1, 2	Praise the Lord, O my soul	Sir John Goss, Mus. D.	165
" cxlvii. 1, 5	O praise the Lord, for it is a good thing	John Weldon	45
" cxlvii. 12 ; cxlviii. 2, 3 ; cvii. 8	Praise the Lord, O Jerusalem	John Scott	46
" cl. 1–4, 6	O praise God in his holiness	John Weldon	47
Isa. xii. 6	Cry aloud, and shout	William Croft, Mus. D.	166
" xxv. 1	O Lord, thou art my God	Sir F. A. Gore Ouseley, Bart., Mus. D.	167
" xxvi. 3	Thou wilt keep him in perfect peace	T. Tallis Trimnell, Mus. B.	168
" lii. 7, 9	How beautiful upon the mountains	R. A. Smith	48
" lx. 1–3	Arise, shine ; for thy light is come	Sir George J. Elvey, Mus. D.	49
" lx. 19, 20	The sun shall be no more thy light by day	A. L. Peace, Mus. D.	104
Jer. v. 24 ; xxxiii. 11	Let us now fear the Lord our God	John Sewell (Bridgnorth)	105
Ezek. xxxvi. 28, 30, 34, 35 ; Ps. cxxxvi. 1 ; Hymn	Ye shall dwell in the land that I gave	Sir John Stainer, M.A., Mus. D.	169
Hosea vi. 1 ; Isa. lv. 7	Come, and let us return unto the Lord	William Jackson (Masham)	50
Micah iv. 2–4	Come, and let us go up	A. L. Peace, Mus. D.	106
Joel ii. 13	Rend your heart, and not your garments	J. Baptiste Calkin	51
Mal. i. 11	From the rising of the sun	Sir F. A. Gore Ouseley, Bart., Mus. D.	170
Tobit viii. 15–17 ; Ps. xx. 2, 4, 1	O God, thou art worthy to be praised	Sir Arthur S. Sullivan, Mus. D.	171
Various texts	Honour and glory, dominion, power	Johann Christian Heinrich Rinck	52

WORDS FROM THE NEW TESTAMENT

Matt. ii. 1, 2 ; Luke i. 32, 33	Now when Jesus was born in Bethlehem	J. L. Hatton	172
" v. 7, 3, 8	Blessed are the merciful	Henry Hiles, Mus. D.	173
" v. 10	Blessed are they which are persecuted	A. L. Peace, Mus. D.	174
" xi. 28, 29	Come unto me, all ye that labour	S. P. Tuckerman, Mus. D.	53
" xi. 28, 29	Come unto me, all ye that labour	H. R. Couldrey	175
" xxiv. 13	He that shall endure to the end	Mendelssohn	107
Luke i. 46–55	My soul doth magnify the Lord	A. L. Peace, Mus. D.	54
" i. 46–55	My soul doth magnify the Lord	Benjamin Cooke, Mus. D.	108
" i. 46–55	My soul doth magnify the Lord	Henry Smart	109
" i. 46–55	My soul doth magnify the Lord	A. L. Peace, Mus. D.	176
" i. 46–55	My soul doth magnify the Lord	Sir George J. Elvey, Mus. D.	177

INDEX OF TEXTS. xiii

WORDS.	FIRST LINE.	COMPOSER OR SOURCE.	NO.
Luke i. 46-55...	My soul doth magnify the Lord...	Sir John Stainer, M.A., Mus. D.	178
" i. 68 70	Blessed be the Lord God of Israel	A. L. Peace, Mus. D.	110
" i. 68-79...	Blessed be the Lord God of Israel	Rev. J. B. Dykes, Mus. D.	179
" i. 68-79...	Blessed be the Lord God of Israel	G. M. Garrett, M.A., Mus. D.	180
" i. 68-79...	Blessed be the Lord God of Israel	Sir John Stainer, M.A., Mus. D.	181
" ii. 8-15 (Metrical)...	While shepherds watched their flocks by night	W. T. Best	210
" ii. 10, 11	Behold, I bring you good tidings	W. H. Gill	55
" ii. 10, 11	Behold, I bring you good tidings	Sir John Goss, Mus. D	182
" ii. 15, 10, 11	Let us now go even unto Bethlehem	J. L. Hatton	111
" ii. 15, 10, 11	Let us now go even unto Bethlehem	E. J. Hopkins, Mus. D.	183
" ii. 29-32	Lord, now lettest thou thy servant	A. L. Peace, Mus. D.	56
" ii. 29-32	Lord, now lettest thou thy servant	Charles King, Mus. B	57
" ii. 29-32	Lord, now lettest thou thy servant	Thomas Ebdon	112
" ii. 29-32	Lord, now lettest thou thy servant	Sir John Goss, Mus. D.	184
" xv. 18, 19	I will arise, and go to my Father	Rev. Richard Cecil	58
" xv. 18, 19	I will arise, and go to my Father	Rev. Richard Cecil Harmonized and arranged by William Jackson	59
" xviii. 16, 17	Suffer little children to come unto me	A. L. Peace, Mus. D.	60
" xxiii. 28	Daughters of Jerusalem	Sir George J. Elvey, Mus. D.	185
" xxiv. 5-7	Why seek ye the living among the dead?	E. J. Hopkins, Mus. D.	186
John iii. 16, 17	God so loved the world	Sir John Goss, Mus. D.	187
" iv. 24, 23	God is a Spirit	Sir W. Sterndale Bennett, Mus. D.	188
" viii. 56; Num. xxiv. 17; Isa. xxvi. 4...	Abraham foresaw the gospel day	William Spark, Mus. D.	83
" xiv. 15-17	If ye love me, keep my commandments	Thomas Tallis	61
" xiv. 15-17, 27	If ye love me, keep my commandments	Sir Robert P. Stewart, Mus. D	189
Rom. vi. 9-11	Christ being raised from the dead	W. H. Gill	62
" xiii. 11, 12	It is high time to awake out of sleep	Joseph Barnby	190
" xiii. 12	The night is far spent	Thomas Hewlett, Mus. B.	63
" xiv. 11, 12; ii. 6, 11; viii. 14; xiv. 7, 8; xi. 33, 36	As I live, saith the Lord	E. T. Chipp, Mus. D.	191
1 Cor. v. 7, 8	Christ our passover is sacrificed for us	Sir John Goss, Mus. D.	192
1 Cor. xv. 20; Rom. vi. 10	Christ is risen from the dead	Sir George J. Elvey, Mus. D.	193
2 Cor. v. 20; Rom. x. 15, 18	Now we are ambassadors in the name... How lovely are the messengers	Mendelssohn	113
1 Thess. iv. 14, 13	If we believe that Jesus died	Sir John Goss, Mus. D.	194
1 Pet. i. 3-5, 15, 17, 22-25	Blessed be the God and Father	S. S. Wesley, Mus. D.	195
Jude 24, 25	Now unto him that is able to keep us from falling	Lowell Mason, Mus. D.	64
Rev. v. 13	And every creature that is in heaven... Blessing, honour, glory, and power	Spohr	114
" vii. 12	Blessing, and glory, and wisdom	William Boyce, Mus. D.	196
" vii. 13-17	Hallelujah! What are these that are arrayed?	Sir John Stainer, M.A., Mus. D.	197
" xiv. 13	Blest are the departed	Spohr	198

WORDS FROM VARIOUS SOURCES.

A Prayer	Lord, for thy tender mercies' sake	Richard Farrant, Mus. B. Also ascribed to John Hilton, Mus. B.	65
Burial Service	Thou knowest, Lord, the secrets of our hearts	Henry Purcell	66
Agnus Dei	Lamb of God, that takest away	J. G. Naumann. Adapted to English words by A. L. Peace, Mus. D.	67
Agnus Dei	Lord, have mercy upon us	J. G. Naumann. Adapted to English words by A. L. Peace, Mus. D.	115
Ave Maria	O Lord, we pray thee	Donizetti. Adapted to English words by A. L. Peace, Mus. D.	116
Ave Maria	O Lord, most holy, O God most mighty	Franz Abt	199
Collect	Grant, we beseech thee, merciful Lord	John Wall Callcott, Mus. D	68
Collect	Lord of all power and might	S. S. Wesley, Mus. D.	69
Collect	Almighty and everlasting God	Orlando Gibbons, Mus. D.	200
Collect	Almighty and merciful God	Sir John Goss, Mus. D.	203
Collect	O Saviour of the world	Sir John Goss, Mus. D.	202
Liturgy	Give peace in our time, O Lord	W. Hutchins Callcott	201
Sanctus	Holy, holy, holy Lord God of hosts	Thomas Attwood	70
Sanctus	Holy, holy, holy Lord God of hosts	Sir George J. Elvey, Mus. D.	71
Sanctus	Holy, holy, holy Lord God of sabaoth	James S. Geikie	72
Sanctus	Holy, holy, holy Lord God of hosts	G. B. Allegri	73
Sanctus	Holy, holy, holy Lord God of hosts	John Camidge, Mus. D.	74
Sanctus	Holy, holy, holy Lord God of hosts	Orlando Gibbons, Mus. D.	75
Sanctus	Holy, holy; thou, O Lord, alone art holy	From a Sanctus in Kocher's Zionsharfe, 1855	76
Sanctus	Holy, holy, holy is God our Lord	Spohr	117

INDEX OF TOPICS.

WORDS.	FIRST LINE.	COMPOSER OR SOURCE.	NO.
Sanctus and Hosanna	Holy, holy, holy: holy art thou	William Russell, Mus. B	118
Te Deum Laudamus	We praise thee, O God	William Jackson (Exeter)	77
Te Deum Laudamus	We praise thee, O God	Sir John Goss, Mus. D	78
Te Deum Laudamus	We praise thee, O God	A. L. Peace, Mus. D	119
Te Deum Laudamus	*We praise thee, O God*	Rev. J. B. Dykes, Mus. D	*204*
Te Deum Laudamus	*We praise thee, O God*	A. L. Peace, Mus. D	*205*
Te Deum Laudamus	*We praise thee, O God*	Henry Smart	*206*
Apostles' Creed	I believe in God the Father Almighty	E. J. Hopkins, Mus. D	*207*
Nicene Creed	*I believe in one God, the Father Almighty*	Sir John Goss, Mus. D	*208*

METRICAL WORDS.

Ps. xviii. 9, 10	The Lord descended from above	Philip Hayes, Mus. D	8
" xlii. 1, 2	As pants the hart for cooling streams	Spohr. Arranged by James Stimpson	133
" lv. 1–7	Hear my prayer, O God, incline thine ear	Mendelssohn	139
" cxxxvii. 1–4	To thee, great Lord o'er all	Rossini	*209*
Psalm	O Lord, in thee is all my trust	Thomas Causton	81
Luke ii. 8–15	While shepherds watched their flocks by night	W. T. Best	*210*
Ave verum	Jesus, Lord, thou Son eternal	Mozart	79
Ave verum	Jesu, Word of God incarnate	Charles Gounod	80
O Salutaris	O Lord my strength, to thee I pray	Auber	82
Jesu dulcis memoria	Thy memory, O Jesus sweet	Franz G. Bühler. Adapted to English words by A. L. Peace, Mus. D.	120
Hymn	Come, Holy Ghost, our souls inspire	Thomas Attwood	*211*
Hymn	Come, Holy Ghost, our souls inspire	Sir George J. Elvey, Mus. D	*212*
Hymn	The radiant morn hath passed away	Rev. H. H. Woodward, M.A., Mus. B.	*213*
Hymn	From thy love as a Father	Charles Gounod	*214*
Hymn	O Holy Ghost, into our minds	Sir George A. Macfarren	*215*
Hymn	Grant us thy peace, Almighty Lord	Mendelssohn	*216*

Index of Topics.

Anthems, the words only of which are given, are indicated by Italic type.

BENEDICTION.

	NO.
The Lord bless thee, and keep thee	1
Blessed be the Lord God, even the God	25
Now unto him that is able	64
Blessed is the man that feareth	101

BLESSING.

Blessed are they that fear the Lord	*156*
The Lord that made heaven	*157*
Ye shall dwell in the land	*169*
O God, thou art worthy to be praised	*171*
Blessed are the merciful	*173*
Blessed are they which are persecuted	*174*

CHILDREN.

Suffer little children to come unto me	60

CHRISTMAS, OR GLAD TIDINGS.

How beautiful upon the mountains	48
Arise, shine; for thy light is come	49
My soul doth magnify the Lord	54
Behold, I bring you good tidings	55
Lord, now lettest thou thy servant	56
Lord, now lettest thou thy servant	57
I shall see him, but not now	83
My soul doth magnify the Lord	109

My soul doth magnify the Lord	109
Blessed be the Lord God of Israel	110
Let us now go even unto Bethlehem	111
Lord, now lettest thou thy servant	112
Now when Jesus was born	*172*
My soul doth magnify the Lord	*176*
My soul doth magnify the Lord	*177*
My soul doth magnify the Lord	*178*
Blessed be the Lord God of Israel	*179*
Blessed be the Lord God of Israel	*180*
Blessed be the Lord God of Israel	*181*
Behold, I bring you good tidings	*182*
Let us now go even unto Bethlehem	*183*
Lord, now lettest thou thy servant	*184*
While shepherds watched their flocks	*210*

CHURCH, GOD'S HOUSE.

Hear the voice and prayer	2
My voice shalt thou hear	6
O how amiable are thy dwellings	26
O worship the Lord in the beauty	23
O be joyful in the Lord	29
O be joyful in the Lord	30
The Lord is my strength	33
Blessed are they that dwell	93
A day in thy courts	94
O be joyful in the Lord	97
Come, and let us go up	106
How goodly are thy tents, O Jacob	*121*

In Jewry is God known	*142*
O how amiable are thy dwellings	*145*
O how amiable are thy dwellings	*146*
The Lord is great in Zion	*150*
O be joyful in the Lord	*151*
I was glad when they said unto me	*155*
O praise the Lord. Laud ye the name	*158*
Praise the Lord, O my soul	*165*

COMFORT.

The Lord will be a refuge	7
O taste and see how gracious	16
Cast thy burden on the Lord	22
Comfort, O Lord, the soul	27
Righteous art thou, O Lord	36
Righteous art thou, O Lord	37
If ye love me, keep my commandments	61
The Lord is full of compassion	99
The Lord is full of compassion	100
If ye love me, keep my commandments	*189*
If we believe that Jesus died	*194*
Hallelujah! What are these	*197*

CONFIDENCE IN GOD.

The Lord will be a refuge	7
The Lord is my shepherd	10
Unto thee, O Lord, do I lift	11
O taste and see how gracious	16

	NO.
Like as the hart desireth	19
Cast thy burden on the Lord	22
I will lift up mine eyes	38
O Lord, we trust alone in thee	41
The Lord is my shepherd	80
My soul truly waiteth still	90
God is our hope and strength	135
The Lord is my strength and my song	154
Mine eyes look unto thee	162

CREEDS.

I believe in God the Father Almighty	207
I believe in one God, the Father	208

CRY UNTO GOD.

My God, look upon me	9
Incline thine ear to me	14
Hear my prayer, O Lord, and give ear	17
Like as the hart desireth	19
Enter not into judgment	43
Lord, for thy tender mercies' sake	65
Grant, we beseech thee, merciful	68
O Lord, in thee is all my trust	81
Hear my prayer, O God	89
O Lord God of my salvation	95
Turn thee again, O Lord	96
Out of the deep have I called	103
Lord, have mercy upon us	115
Save me, O God, for thy name's sake	138
Hear my prayer, O God	139
I will cry unto God with my voice	143
Bow thine ear, O Lord, and hear	147
Give ear, O Lord, unto my prayer	148
By the waters of Babylon	159
Lord, I call upon thee	160
Lord, I call upon thee	161
O Saviour of the world	202
To thee, great Lord o'er all	209

DOXOLOGY.

Now unto him that is able	64
Blessing, honour, glory, and power	114
Blessing, and glory, and wisdom	196

EARTH'S FERTILITY.

Thou visitest the earth	23
God be merciful unto us	24
O Lord, how manifold are thy works	32
God be merciful unto us	91
Let the people praise thee, O God	92
Let us now fear the Lord our God	105
Thou visitest the earth	141
Ye shall dwell in the land	169

EASTER.

The Lord is my strength and my song	33
Christ being raised from the dead	62
O give thanks unto the Lord; for he	153
The Lord is my strength and my song	154
Why seek ye the living among the	186
Christ, our passover, is sacrificed	192
Christ is risen from the dead	193

ENTREATY TO BE HEARD.

Hear the voice and prayer	2
O Lord my God, hear thou	3

	NO.
Hear me when I call	4
I will lay me down in peace	5
My voice shalt thou hear	6
Hear my prayer, O Lord, and give ear	17
Hear my prayer, O Lord; give ear	42
Lord, hear my prayer	98
O Lord my God, hear thou	122
Call to remembrance thy tender	129
Hear my prayer, O God	139

EVENING.

Hear me when I call	4
I will lay me down in peace	5
I will lay me down in peace	123
I will lay me down in peace	124
The radiant morn hath passed away	213

FORGIVENESS, GOD'S MERCY.

Call to remembrance, O Lord	12
Thou knowest, Lord, the secrets	66
The Lord is full of compassion	99
The Lord is full of compassion	100
Call to remembrance thy tender	129
O God, thou art worthy to be praised	171
God so loved the world	187

GOD ABIDING.

O Lord, thy word endureth for ever	35

GOD'S KINGDOM.

From the rising of the sun	170
Now when Jesus was born	172
Hallelujah! What are these	197

GOD'S PRESENCE.

The Lord will be a refuge	7
The Lord descended from above	8
I will lift up mine eyes	38

HEAVEN.

The sun shall be no more thy light	104
Hallelujah! What are these	197
Blest are the departed	198
The radiant morn hath passed away	213
From thy love as a Father	214

HELPING THE POOR.

Blessed is he that considereth the poor	18

HOSANNA.

Holy, holy, holy: holy art thou	118

HOW LONG, O LORD.

Lord, how long wilt thou forget me?	126
Hear, O thou Shepherd of Israel	144
Bow thine ear, O Lord, and hear	147

INVITATION.

O taste and see how gracious	16
Come unto me, all ye that labour	53
Suffer little children to come unto me	60
Come unto me, all ye that labour	175

JOY.

	NO.
Rejoice in the Lord, O ye righteous	15
God be merciful unto us	24
O be joyful in the Lord, all ye lands	29
O be joyful in the Lord, all ye lands	30
God be merciful unto us	91
O be joyful in the Lord, all ye lands	97
My soul doth magnify the Lord	108
My soul doth magnify the Lord	109
O clap your hands together, all ye	136
O be joyful in the Lord, all ye lands	151
O give thanks unto the Lord, and call	152
Cry aloud and shout	166
O God, thou art worthy to be praised	171
My soul doth magnify the Lord	176
My soul doth magnify the Lord	177
My soul doth magnify the Lord	178

KING OF GLORY.

Lift up your heads, O ye gates	128
The Lord is great in Zion	150
The Lord is loving unto every man	164

MARRIAGE.

God be merciful unto us	24
Blessed are they that fear the Lord	156
O God, thou art worthy to be praised	171

MORNING.

My voice shalt thou hear	6

OBEDIENCE.

Teach me, O Lord, the way	34
Righteous art thou, O Lord	37
If ye love me, keep my commandments	61
Lord of all power and might	69
If ye love me, keep my commandments	189

PEACE.

The Lord bless thee, and keep thee	1
Hear me when I call	4
I will lay me down in peace	5
Pray for the peace of Jerusalem	39
Lord, now lettest thou thy servant	56
Lord, now lettest thou thy servant	57
Come, and let us go up	106
Lord, now lettest thou thy servant	112
Now we are ambassadors in the name	113
How lovely are the messengers	113
I was glad when they said unto me	155
Praise the Lord, O my soul	165
Thou wilt keep him in perfect peace	168
Lord, now lettest thou thy servant	184
If ye love me, keep my commandments	189
Give peace in our time, O Lord	201
Grant us thy peace, Almighty Lord	216

PENITENCE.

I will wash my hands in innocency	13
Turn thy face from my sins	20
Create in me a clean heart, O God	21
Come, and let us return unto the Lord	50
Rend your heart, and not your	51
I will arise, and go to my Father	58
I will arise, and go to my Father	59

INDEX OF TOPICS.

	NO.
The night is far spent	63
O Lord God of my salvation	95
The Lord is full of compassion	100
Out of the deep have I called	103
Thy memory, O Jesus sweet	120
The sacrifices of God are a broken	137
Daughters of Jerusalem	185
It is high time to awake out of sleep	190

PERSEVERANCE.

Lord, for thy tender mercies' sake	65
Lord of all power and might	69
O love the Lord, all ye his saints	87
He that shall endure to the end	107

PRAISE FOR HELP.

We praise thee, O God	77
We praise thee, O God	78
We praise thee, O God	119
Hear, O Lord, and have mercy	130
I waited for the Lord	132
It is a good thing to give thanks	149
Blessed are they that fear the Lord	156
I will magnify thee, O God, my king	163
O Lord, thou art my God	167
We praise thee, O God	204
We praise thee, O God	205
We praise thee, O God	206

PRAISE OF GOD FROM NATURE.

Thou visitest the earth	23
Blessed be the Lord God, even	25
Praise the Lord, O Jerusalem	46
O praise God in his holiness	47
Blessed be thou, Lord God of Israel	84
Let the people praise thee, O God	92
Let us now fear the Lord our God	105
Thou visitest the earth	141

PRAYER FOR HELP.

O Lord, my God, hear thou the prayer	3
Incline thine ear to me	14
Turn thy face from my sins	20
Create in me a clean heart, O God	21
God be merciful unto us	24
Lord, for thy tender mercies' sake	65
Thou knowest, Lord, the secrets	66
Grant, we beseech thee, merciful Lord	68
O Lord, in thee is all my trust	81
O Lord, my strength, to thee I pray	82
God be merciful unto us	91
Lord, have mercy upon us	115
O Lord, we pray thee	116
O Lord my God, hear thou the prayer	122
Send out thy light and thy truth	134
Hear, O thou Shepherd of Israel	144
Mine eyes look unto thee	163

	NO.
O Lord most holy, O God most mighty	199
Almighty and everlasting God	200
O Saviour of the world	202
Almighty and merciful God	203
To thee, great Lord o'er all	209

PRAYER TO THE SAVIOUR.

Lamb of God, that takest away	67
Jesus, Lord, thou Son eternal	79
Jesu, Word of God incarnate	80
Thy memory, O Jesus sweet	120

RESURRECTION.

Christ being raised from the dead	62
If we believe that Jesus died	194
Blessed be the God and Father	195

SELF-EXAMINATION.

I will wash my hands in innocency	13
How dear are thy counsels unto me	40

SONGS OF PRAISE.

Unto thee, O Lord, do I lift up	11
O be joyful in the Lord, all ye lands	29
O be joyful in the Lord, all ye lands	30
My song shall be of mercy	31
I will extol thee, my God, O King	44
O praise the Lord, for it is a good	45
Honour and glory, dominion, power	52
My soul doth magnify the Lord	54
We praise thee, O God	77
We praise thee, O God	78
I will sing of the Lord	85
O be joyful in the Lord, all ye lands	97
My soul doth magnify the Lord	108
My soul doth magnify the Lord	109
Blessed be the Lord God of Israel	110
We praise thee, O God	119
O be joyful in the Lord, all ye lands	151
My soul doth magnify the Lord	176
My soul doth magnify the Lord	177
My soul doth magnify the Lord	178
Blessed be the Lord God of Israel	179
Blessed be the Lord God of Israel	180
Blessed be the Lord God of Israel	181
We praise thee, O God	204
We praise thee, O God	205
We praise thee, O God	206

SPIRITUAL LONGING.

Like as the hart desireth	19
O how amiable are thy dwellings	26
As pants the hart for cooling streams	133
O how amiable are thy dwellings	145
O how amiable are thy dwellings	146

TER SANCTUS.

	NO.
Holy, holy, holy Lord God of hosts	70
Holy, holy, holy Lord God of hosts	71
Holy, holy, holy Lord God of sabaoth	72
Holy, holy, holy Lord God of hosts	73
Holy, holy, holy Lord God of hosts	74
Holy, holy, holy Lord God of hosts	75
Holy, holy: thou, O Lord, alone	76
Holy, holy, holy is God our Lord	117
Holy, holy, holy: holy art thou	118

THANKS AND THANKSGIVING.

Rejoice in the Lord, O ye righteous	15
We praise thee, O God	77
We praise thee, O God	78
I will alway give thanks	83
O praise the Lord, all ye nations	102
We praise thee, O God	119
Awake up, my glory	140
It is a good thing to give thanks	149
O give thanks unto the Lord, and call	152
O give thanks unto the Lord; for he	153
The Lord is my strength and my song	154
O praise the Lord. Laud ye the name	158
I will magnify thee, O God, my King	163
The Lord is loving unto every man	164
Blessed be the God and Father	195
We praise thee, O God	204
We praise thee, O God	205
We praise thee, O God	206

THE COMFORTER.

If ye love me, keep my commandments	61
If ye love me, keep my commandments	189
Come, Holy Ghost, our souls inspire	211
Come, Holy Ghost, our souls inspire	212
O Holy Ghost, into our minds	215

THE JUST MAN.

Lord, who shall dwell in thy	127
Keep innocency, and take heed	131

THE LORD THE JUDGE.

In the Lord put I my trust	125
Keep innocency, and take heed	131
The Lord is loving unto every man	164
As I live, saith the Lord	191

WORSHIP.

O worship the Lord in the beauty	28
The Lord is great in Zion	150
O praise the Lord. Laud ye the name	158
God is a Spirit	188

THE SCOTTISH ANTHEM BOOK.

Anthem 1.

Num. vi. 24-26.   THE LORD BLESS THEE.   *Harmony by Lowell Mason, Mus. D.*

Anthem 2.

HEAR THE VOICE AND PRAYER

Anthem 3.

Anthem 4.

Anthem 4.

HEAR ME WHEN I CALL.

Anthem 4.
HEAR ME WHEN I CALL.

Anthem 5.

I WILL LAY ME DOWN IN PEACE.

Ps. iv. 8.   W. H. Gill.

Anthem 6.

Ps. v. 3, 7 MY VOICE SHALT THOU HEAR

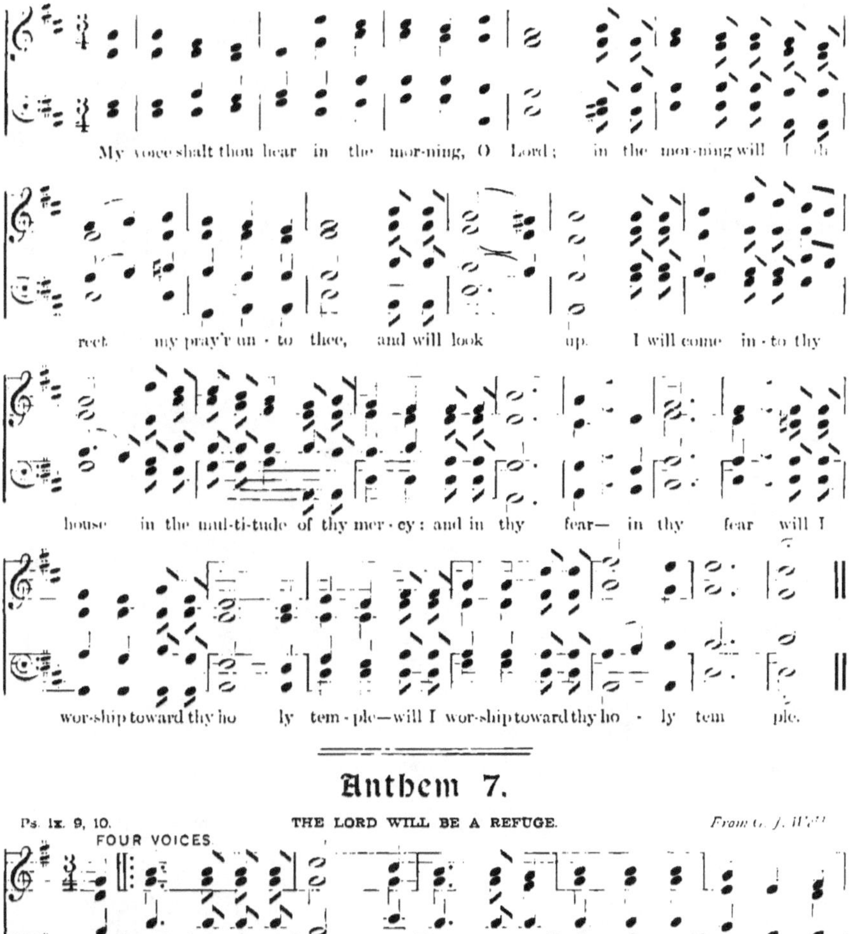

Anthem 7.

Ps. lx. 9, 10. THE LORD WILL BE A REFUGE.

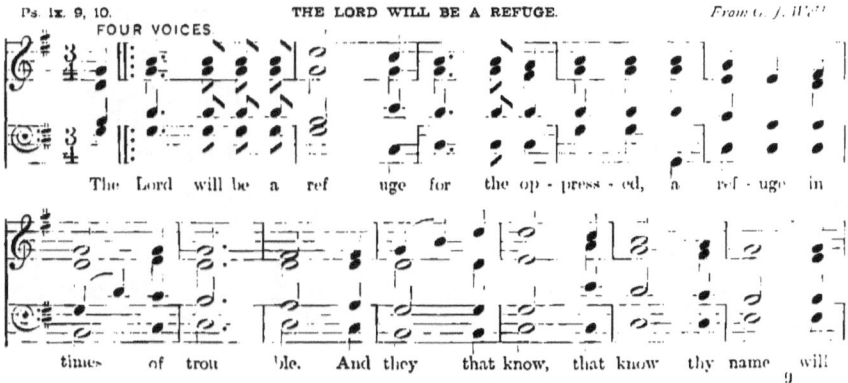

Anthem 7.
THE LORD WILL BE A REFUGE.

Anthem 8.
THE LORD DESCENDED FROM ABOVE.

Anthem 8.
THE LORD DESCENDED FROM ABOVE

Anthem 8.
THE LORD DESCENDED FROM ABOVE.

Anthem 9.

MY GOD, LOOK UPON ME.

Anthem 9.

MY GOD, LOOK UPON ME.

Anthem 9.

MY GOD, LOOK UPON ME.

Anthem 9.

MY GOD, LOOK UPON ME.

Anthem 10.
THE LORD IS MY SHEPHERD.

Anthem 10.

THE LORD IS MY SHEPHERD.

poco rall. e dim.   *a tempo.*

of the sha - dow of death, I will fear no ev - il: for thou art with me; thy

for thou

rod and thy staff, thy rod and thy staff, thy rod and thy staff they

com - fort me, they com - fort me. Sure - ly, sure - ly

Anthem 10.

THE LORD IS MY SHEPHERD.

Anthem II.

Anthem 11.

UNTO THEE, O LORD.

Anthem 11.
UNTO THEE, O LORD.

Anthem 11.
UNTO THEE, O LORD.

26

Anthem 11.

UNTO THEE, O LORD.

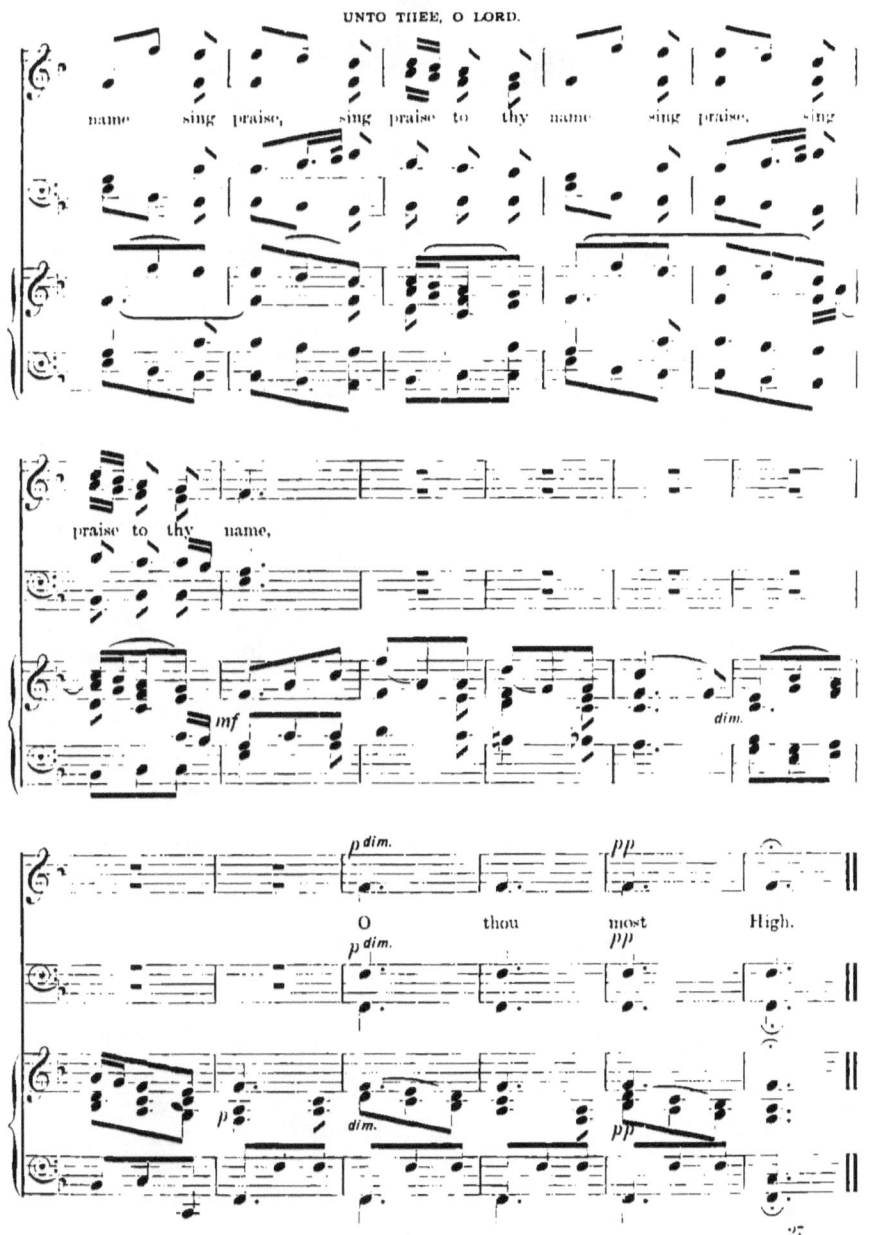

Anthem 13.

I WILL WASH MY HANDS IN INNOCENCY

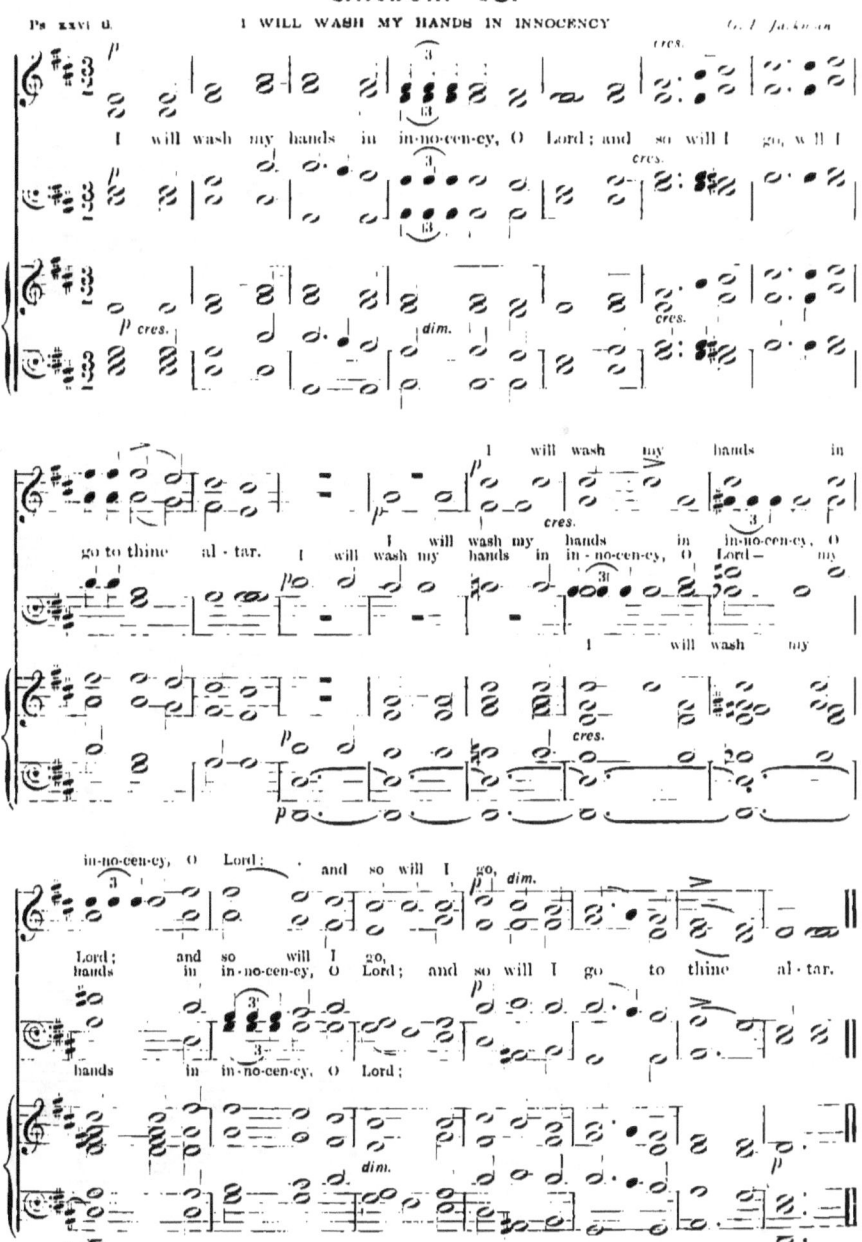

Anthem 14.

Ps. xxxi. 2, 16.   INCLINE THINE EAR TO ME.   F. H. Himmel.
Adapted by William Patten.

Anthem 14.

INCLINE THINE EAR TO ME.

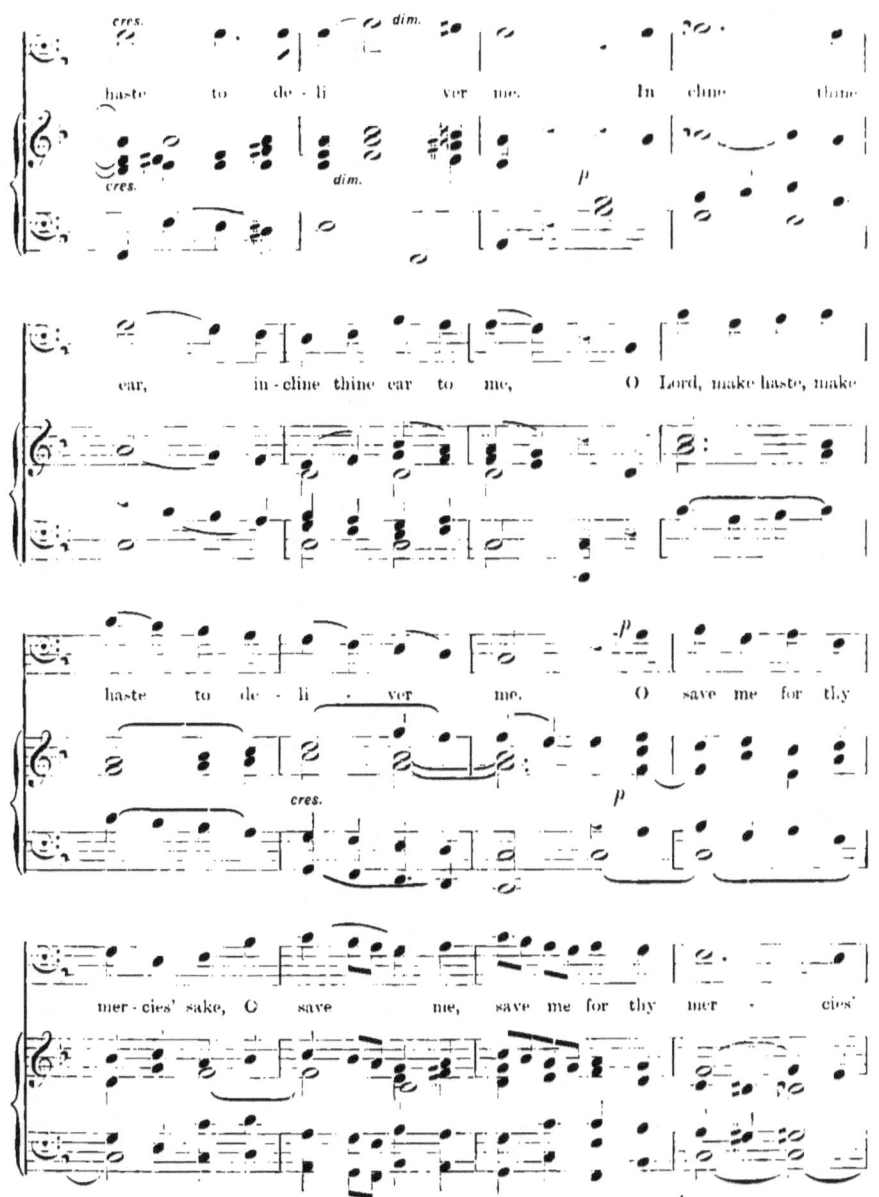

Anthem 14.
INCLINE THINE EAR TO ME.

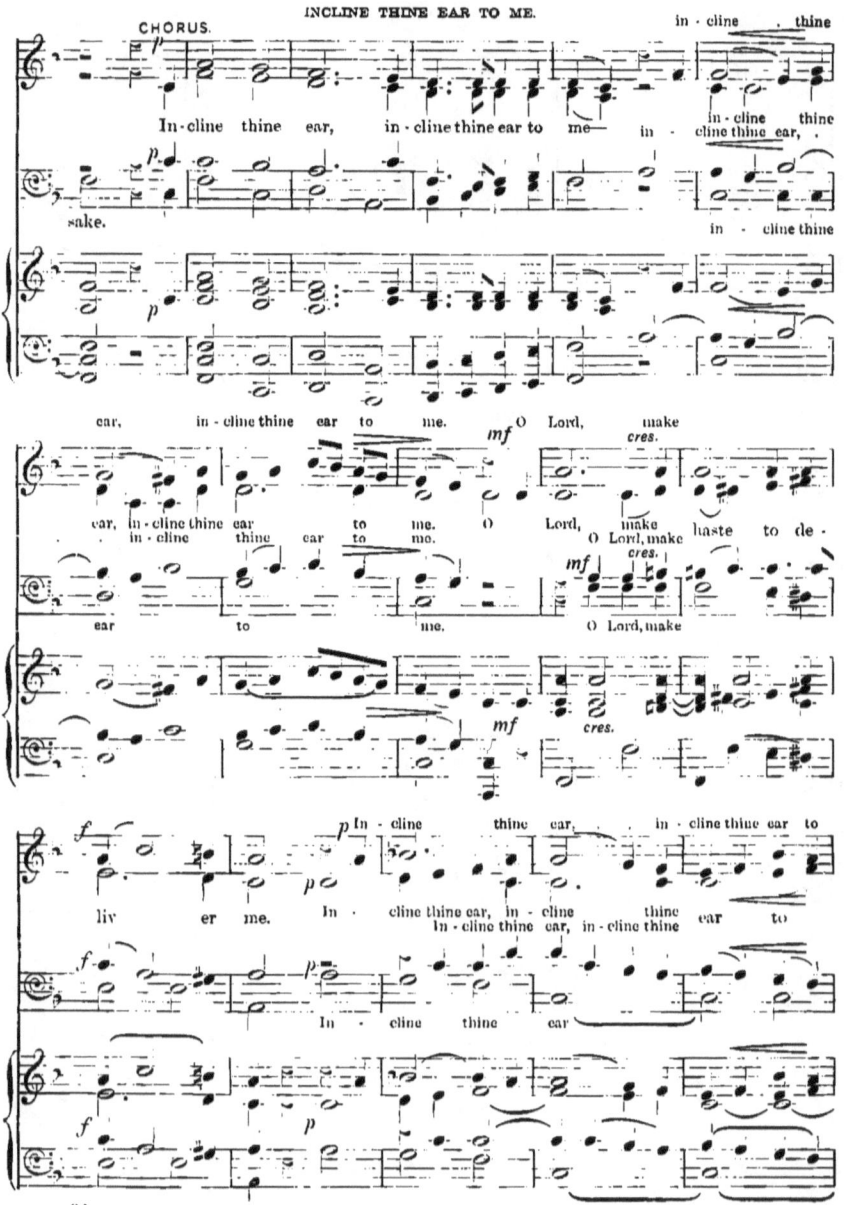

Anthem 14.
INCLINE THINE EAR TO ME

Anthem 15.

REJOICE IN THE LORD.

Anthem 15.

REJOICE IN THE LORD.

Anthem 16.

O TASTE AND SEE.

Anthem 16.

O TASTE AND SEE.

Anthem 16.

O TASTE AND SEE.

Anthem 16.

O TASTE AND SEE.

Anthem 17.
HEAR MY PRAYER, O LORD.

Anthem 17.
HEAR MY PRAYER, O LORD.

44

Anthem 18.

Anthem 18.

BLESSED IS HE THAT CONSIDERETH THE POOR.

Anthem 18.

BLESSED IS HE THAT CONSIDERETH THE POOR

47

Anthem 20.

TURN THY FACE FROM MY SINS.

Anthem 20.
TURN THY FACE FROM MY SINS.

Anthem 20.

TURN THY FACE FROM MY SINS.

Anthem 21.

Ps. li. 10-13. **CREATE IN ME A CLEAN HEART, O GOD.** *Ebenezer Prout, B.A.*

Anthem 21.

CREATE IN ME A CLEAN HEART, O GOD.

Anthem 23.

Ps. lxv. 0, 11. THOU VISITEST THE EARTH. *Maurice Greene, Mus. D.*

Anthem 23.

THOU VISITEST THE EARTH.

56

Anthem 23.
THOU VISITEST THE EARTH.

Anthem 24.

GOD BE MERCIFUL UNTO US.

Anthem 25.

BLESSED BE THE LORD GOD.

Anthem 26.

O HOW AMIABLE ARE THY DWELLINGS.

Anthem 27.

Ps. lxxxvi. 4.   COMFORT, O LORD, THE SOUL OF THY SERVANT.   *William Crotch, Mus. D.*

Anthem 27.

COMFORT, O LORD, THE SOUL OF THY SERVANT.

Anthem 28.
O WORSHIP THE LORD.

Anthem 29.

O BE JOYFUL IN THE LORD. *Samuel Sebastian Wesley, Mus. D.*

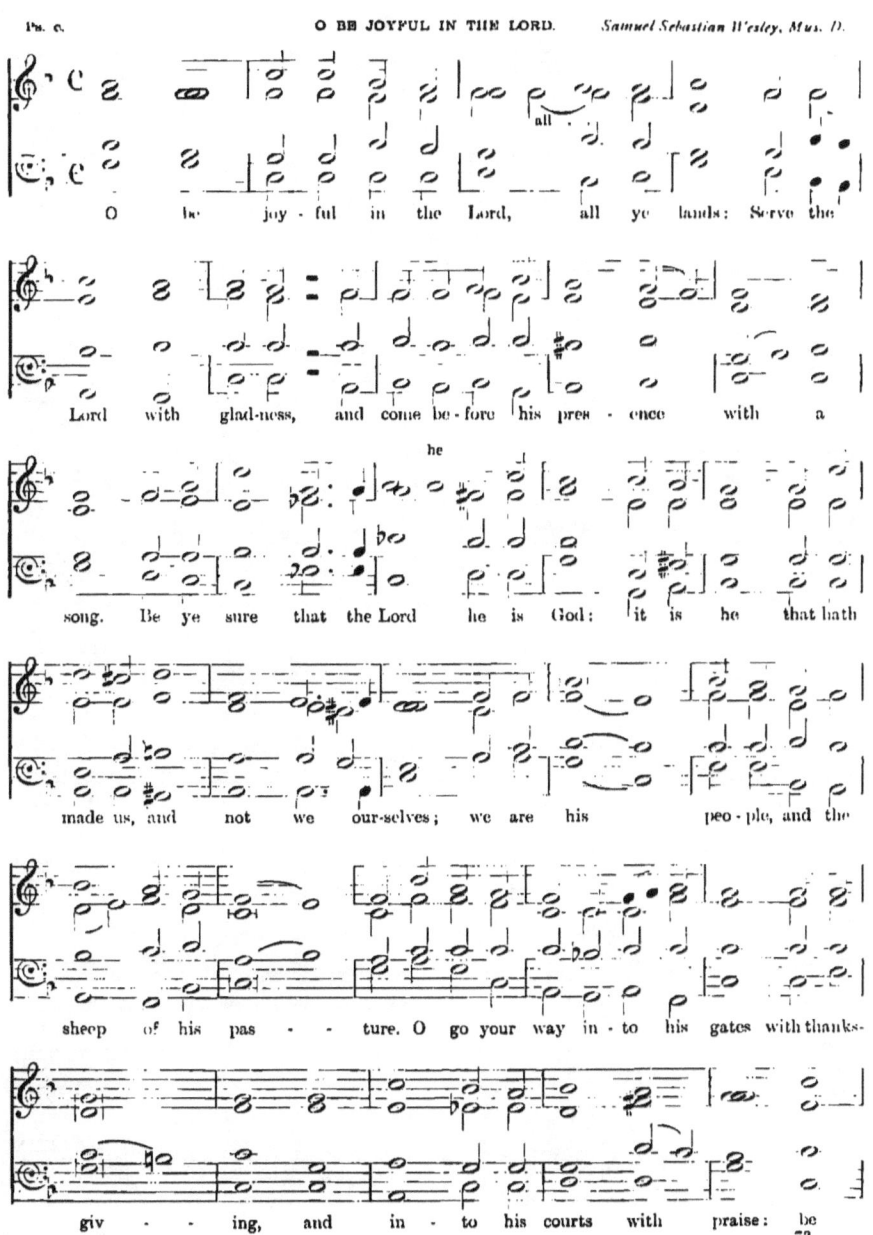

Anthem 30.

O BE JOYFUL IN THE LORD.

J. Clarke-Whitfeld, Mus. D.

Anthem 30.

O BE JOYFUL IN THE LORD.

Anthem 30.

O BE JOYFUL IN THE LORD.

be thank-ful un-to him, and speak good of his name.

For the Lord is gra-cious; his mer-cy is ev-er-last-ing; and his truth, his truth en-dur-eth from gen-er-a-tion to gen-er-a-tion.

Anthem 30.
O BE JOYFUL IN THE LORD.

Anthem 31.

MY SONG SHALL BE OF MERCY

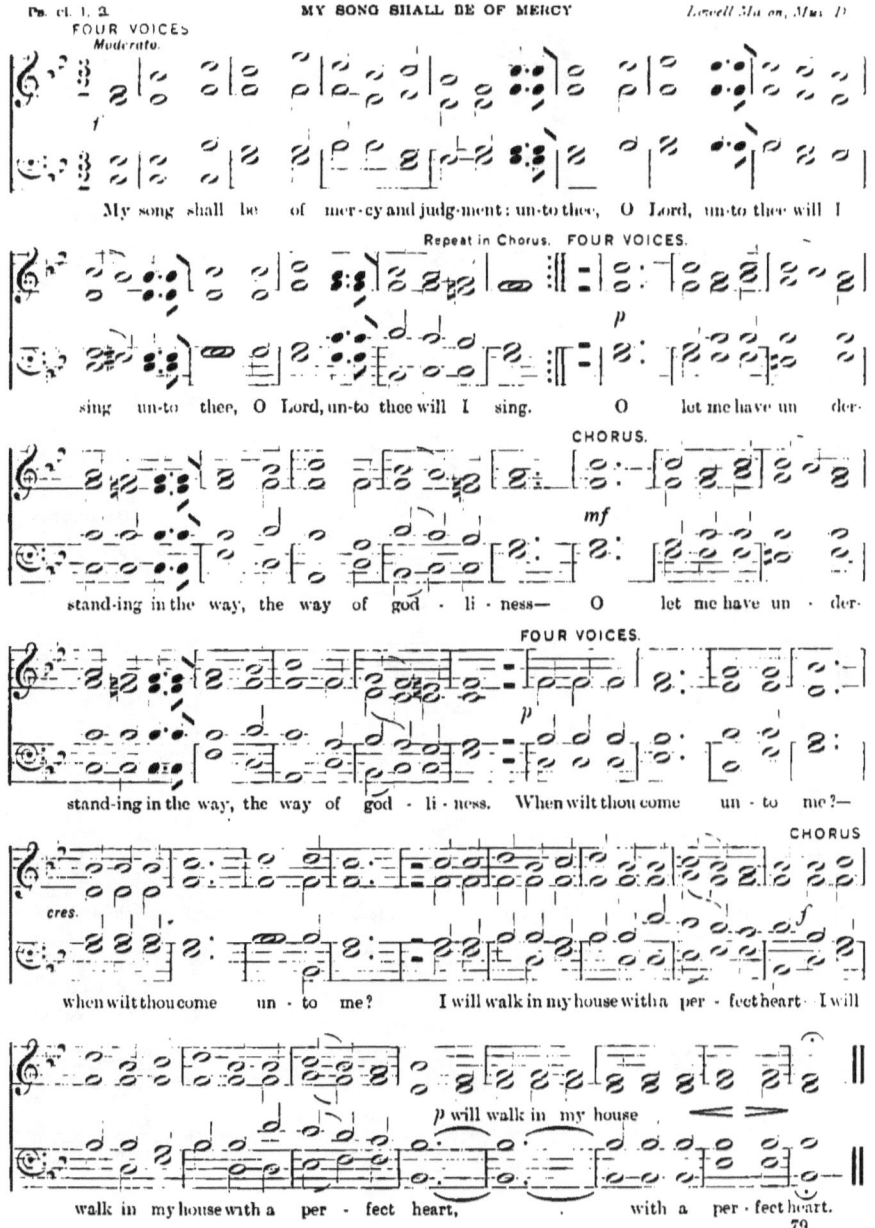

Anthem 32.

O LORD, HOW MANIFOLD ARE THY WORKS.

Anthem 32.

O LORD, HOW MANIFOLD ARE THY WORKS.

Anthem 32.

O LORD, HOW MANIFOLD ARE THY WORKS.

Anthem 32.

O LORD, HOW MANIFOLD ARE THY WORKS.

Anthem 33.

Ps. cxviii 14, 19, 22, 24.   THE LORD IS MY STRENGTH AND MY SONG   W. H. Monk, Mus. D.

85

Anthem 33.

THE LORD IS MY STRENGTH AND MY SONG.

Anthem 33.

THE LORD IS MY STRENGTH AND MY SONG.

Anthem 34.

Ps. cxix. 33.   TEACH ME, O LORD, THE WAY OF THY STATUTES.   *Thomas Attwood.*

Anthem 34.

TEACH ME, O LORD, THE WAY OF THY STATUTES.

Anthem 34.

TEACH ME, O LORD, THE WAY OF THY STATUTES.

Anthem 35.

Ps. cxix. 89-91. O LORD, THY WORD ENDURETH. *Christopher Tye, Mus. D.*

Anthem 36.

Ps. cxix 137, 142, 143 — RIGHTEOUS ART THOU, O LORD. — Philip Hayes, Mus. D.

TWO TREBLES

Anthem 36.
RIGHTEOUS ART THOU, O LORD.

Anthem 36.
RIGHTEOUS ART THOU, O LORD.

Anthem 37.

RIGHTEOUS ART THOU, O LORD.

Anthem 37.
RIGHTEOUS ART THOU, O LORD

Anthem 37.

RIGHTEOUS ART THOU, O LORD.

Anthem 38.

I WILL LIFT UP MINE EYES.

Anthem 38.

I WILL LIFT UP MINE EYES.

Anthem 38.

I WILL LIFT UP MINE EYES.

Anthem 38.

I WILL LIFT UP MINE EYES

Anthem 39.

Anthem 40.
HOW DEAR ARE THY COUNSELS.

Anthem 41.

O LORD, WE TRUST ALONE IN THEE.

Anthem 42.

HEAR MY PRAYER, O LORD.

Anthem 42.

HEAR MY PRAYER, O LORD.

Anthem 43.

Anthem 43.

ENTER NOT INTO JUDGMENT.

Anthem 44.

I WILL EXTOL THEE, MY GOD, O KING.

Anthem 45.

Ps. cxlvii. 1, 5. O PRAISE THE LORD. *John Weldon.*

114

Anthem 46.

Ps. cxlvii. 12; cxlviii. 2, 3; cvii. 8 PRAISE THE LORD, O JERUSALEM. *John Scott.*

Anthem 46.

PRAISE THE LORD, O JERUSALEM.

Anthem 46.

PRAISE THE LORD, O JERUSALEM.

Anthem 47.

Anthem 48.

Isa. lii. 7, 9.   HOW BEAUTIFUL UPON THE MOUNTAINS.   R. A. Smith.

Anthem 48.

HOW BEAUTIFUL UPON THE MOUNTAINS.

Anthem 49.

Isa. lx. 1-3. ARISE, SHINE. Sir George J. Elvey, Mus. D.

Anthem 49.

ARISE, SHINE.

Anthem 49.

ARISE, SHINE.

Anthem 49.

ARISE, SHINE.

Anthem 50.

Anthem 50.

COME, AND LET US RETURN.

Anthem 52.
HONOUR AND GLORY.

Anthem 54.

Luke i. 46-55. MY SOUL DOTH MAGNIFY THE LORD. A. L. Peace, Mus. D.

Anthem 54.
MY SOUL DOTH MAGNIFY THE LORD.

Anthem 54.
MY SOUL DOTH MAGNIFY THE LORD.

Anthem 54.

MY SOUL DOTH MAGNIFY THE LORD.

Anthem 54.

MY SOUL DOTH MAGNIFY THE LORD.

Anthem 54.

MY SOUL DOTH MAGNIFY THE LORD.

Anthem 55.

BEHOLD, I BRING YOU GOOD TIDINGS.

Anthem 56.

Luke ii. 29-32. **LORD, NOW LETTEST THOU.** A. L. Peace, Mus. D.

Anthem 56.

LORD, NOW LETTEST THOU.

Anthem 56.

LORD, NOW LETTEST THOU.

Anthem 56.

LORD, NOW LETTEST THOU.

Anthem 56.
LORD, NOW LETTEST THOU.

Anthem 56.

LORD, NOW LETTEST THOU.

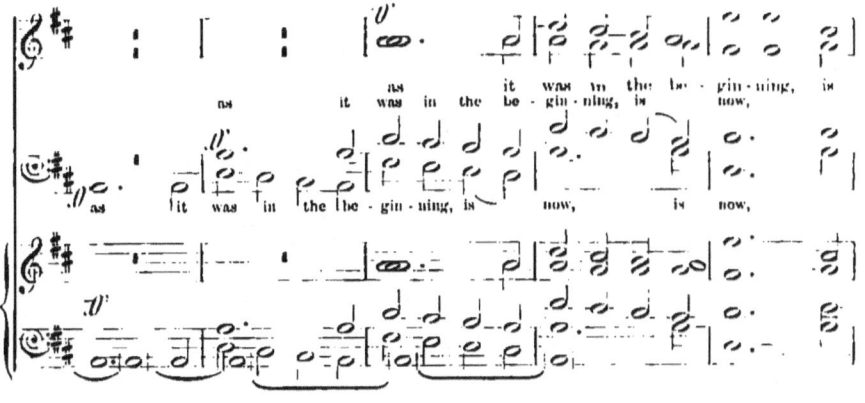

Anthem 57.

LORD, NOW LETTEST THOU.

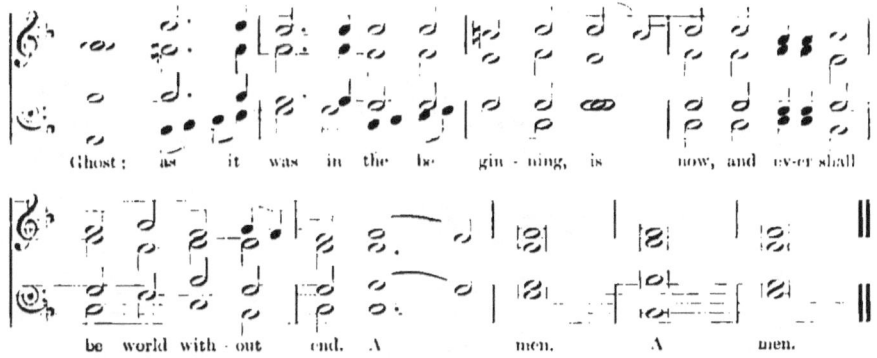

Ghost: as it was in the be - gin - ning, is now, and ev-er shall be world with-out end. A - men. A - men.

Anthem 58.

Luke xv. 18, 19.   **I WILL ARISE.**   Rev. Richard Cecil.

Andante.

ORGAN. *p*

cres.

[A. L. P.]

I will a - rise, I will a - rise and go to my fa - ther, and will say un - to

Anthem 58.

I WILL ARISE.

him, Fa - ther, fa - ther, I have sin - ned, have sin - ned, I have sin-ned a-gainst heav'n, and be - fore thee, and am no more wor - thy to be call - ed thy son— I will a - rise, I will a - rise and go to my fa - ther, my fa - ther.

Anthem 59.

Luke xv. 18, 19.
Andante.
I WILL ARISE.
Rev. Richard Cecil. Harmonized and arranged by William Jackson.
[A. L. P.]

Anthem 59.

I WILL ARISE.

Anthem 60.
SUFFER LITTLE CHILDREN

suffer little children to come un to me, and for-bid them not, forbid them not: for of such is the kingdom, the kingdom of God.

Anthem 60.
SUFFER LITTLE CHILDREN.

Anthem 60.
SUFFER LITTLE CHILDREN

Suf-fer lit-tle chil-dren to come un-to me, and for-bid them not, for-bid them not: for of such is the king-dom of God— suf-fer lit-tle chil-dren to come un-to me, suf-fer lit-tle chil-dren to

Anthem 60.
SUFFER LITTLE CHILDREN.

Anthem 61.

John xiv 16-17.   IF YE LOVE ME, KEEP MY COMMANDMENTS   Thomas Tallis

Anthem 61.

IF YE LOVE ME, KEEP MY COMMANDMENTS.

* *The small notes form the alto part.*

Anthem 62.

Anthem 62.

CHRIST BEING RAISED FROM THE DEAD.

Anthem 63.

THE NIGHT IS FAR SPENT

Anthem 63.
THE NIGHT IS FAR SPENT.

160

Anthem 63.
THE NIGHT IS FAR SPENT

Anthem 65.
LORD, FOR THY TENDER MERCIES' SAKE.

Anthem 66.
THOU KNOWEST, LORD. *Henry Purcell.*

Burial Service.

Anthem 66.

THOU KNOWEST, LORD.

Anthem 67.

LAMB OF GOD.

167

Anthem 67.

LAMB OF GOD.

Anthem 68.

GRANT, WE BESEECH THEE, MERCIFUL LORD. *John Wall Callcott, Mus. D.*

Anthem 68.

GRANT, WE BESEECH THEE, MERCIFUL LORD.

Anthem 68.

GRANT, WE BESEECH THEE, MERCIFUL LORD.

Anthem 69.

LORD OF ALL POWER AND MIGHT — *Samuel Sebastian Wesley*

Anthem 71.

HOLY, HOLY, HOLY LORD GOD OF HOSTS

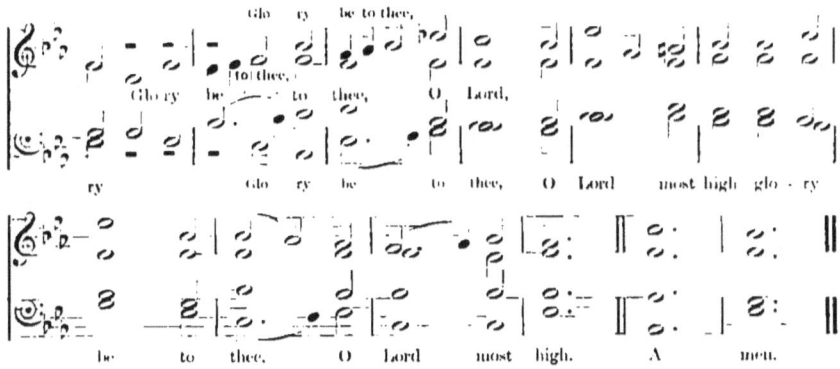

Anthem 72.

HOLY, HOLY, HOLY LORD GOD OF SABAOTH.

Sanctus.   James S. Geikie.

Anthem 73.

Sanctus. HOLY, HOLY, HOLY LORD GOD OF HOSTS. *G. B. Allegri.*

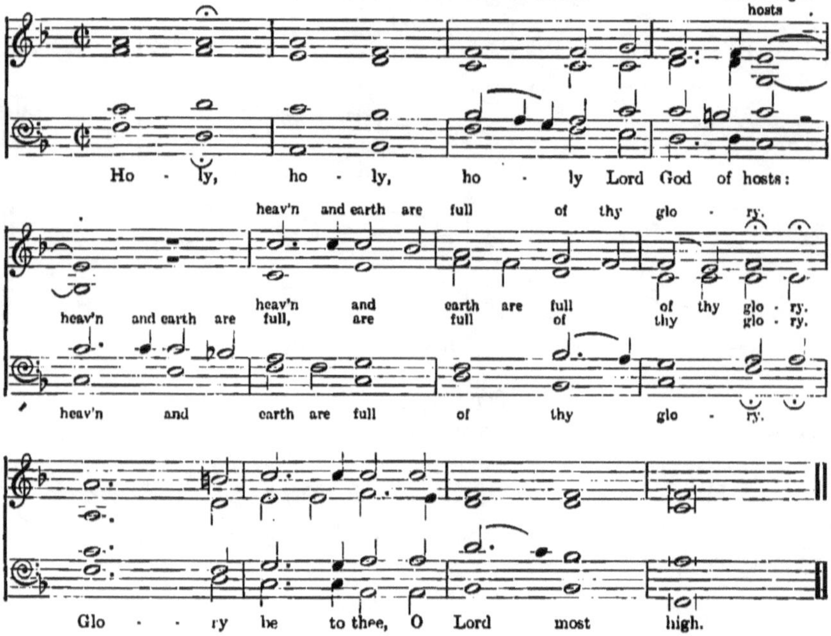

Anthem 74.

Sanctus. HOLY, HOLY, HOLY LORD GOD OF HOSTS. *John Camidge, Mus. D.*

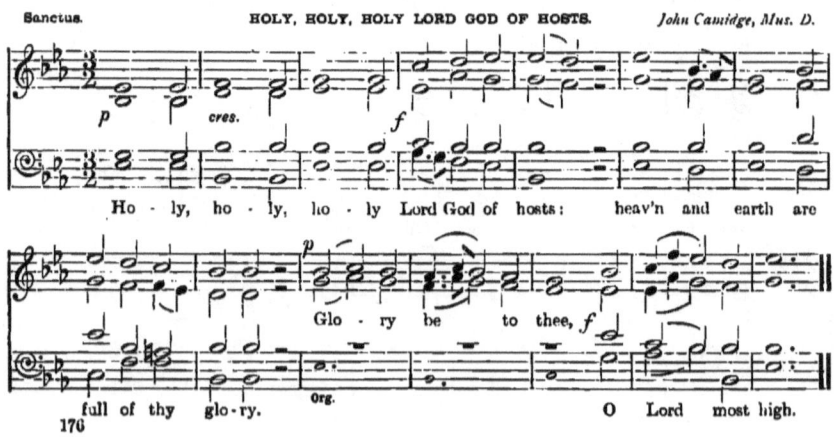

Anthem 75.

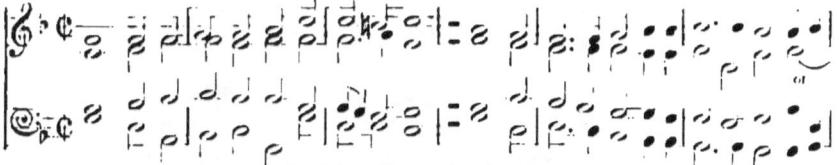

Anthem 76.

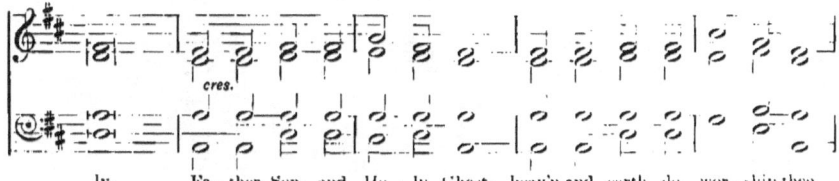

Anthem 77.

WE PRAISE THEE, O GOD.

Anthem 77.

WE PRAISE THEE, O GOD.

Anthem 77.
WE PRAISE THEE, O GOD.

Anthem 78.

WE PRAISE THEE, O GOD.

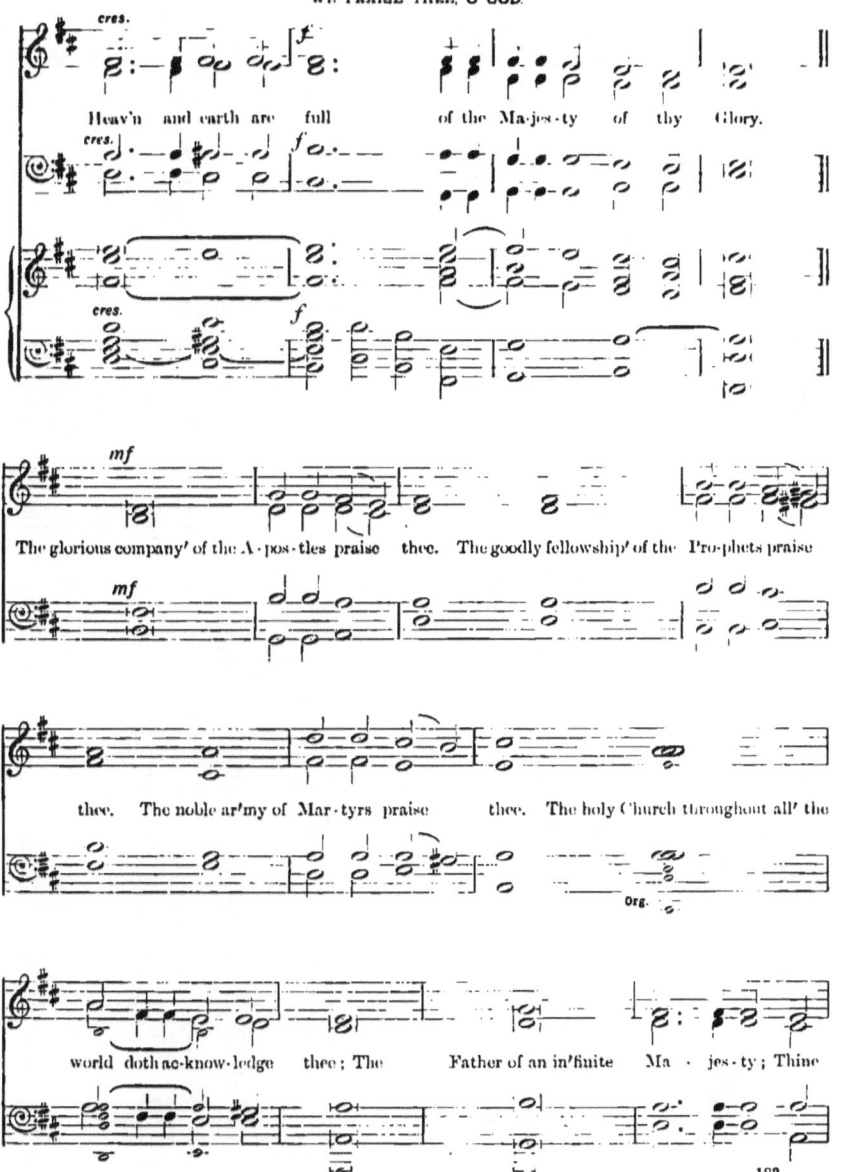

Anthem 78.

WE PRAISE THEE, O GOD.

Anthem 78.
WE PRAISE THEE, O GOD.

Anthem 78.
WE PRAISE THEE, O GOD.

Anthem 79.

JESUS, LORD, THOU SON ETERNAL.

Anthem 79.
JESUS, LORD, THOU SON ETERNAL.

Anthem 79.
JESUS, LORD, THOU SON ETERNAL.

Anthem 80.

Ave verum. — JESU, WORD OF GOD INCARNATE. — *Ch. Gounod.*

Anthem 80.
JESU, WORD OF GOD INCARNATE.

Anthem 81.
O LORD, IN THEE IS ALL MY TRUST.
Thomas Causton.

Anthem 82.

O Salutaris. O LORD, MY STRENGTH. Auber.

O Lord, my strength, to thee I pray; Turn not thou thine ear away: Grant me, Lord, thy love to share; Feed me with a shepherd's care. Thou my rock and fortress art; Thou the refuge of my heart— Thou my rock and fortress art; Thou the refuge of my heart. O Lord, my strength, to thee I pray.

THE SCOTTISH ANTHEM BOOK.

Anthem 83.

I SHALL SEE HIM, BUT NOT NOW.

William Spark, Mus. D.

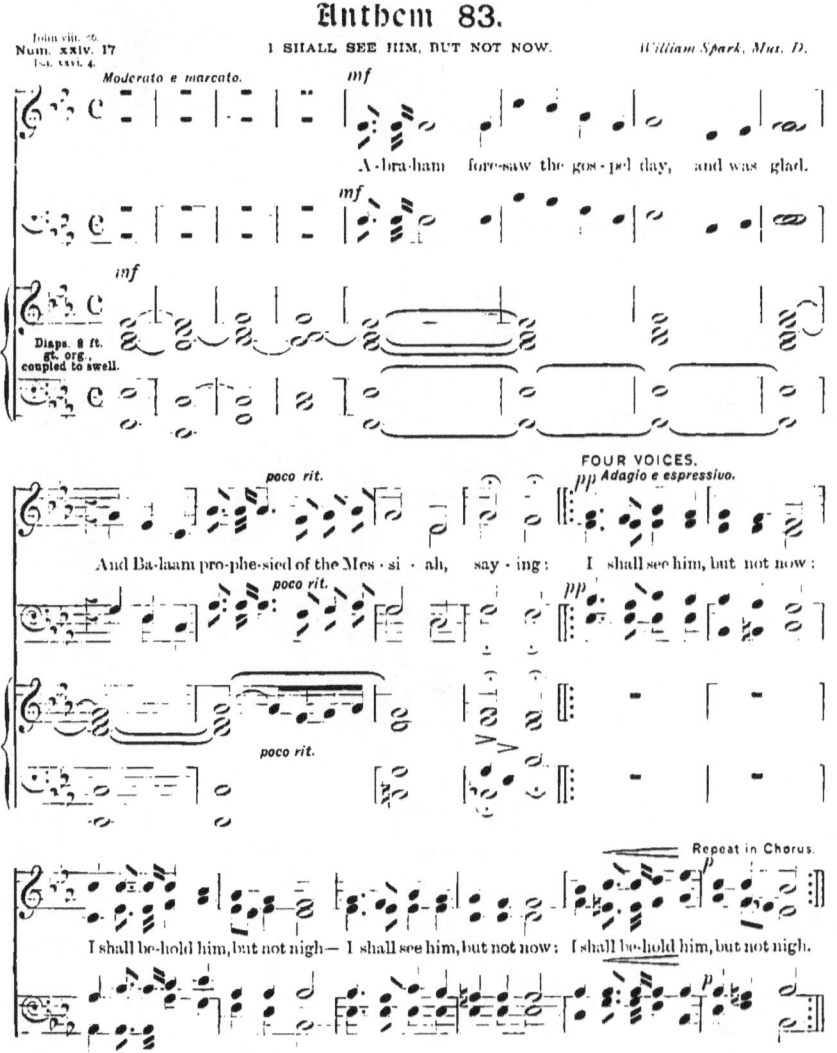

Anthem 83.

I SHALL SEE HIM, BUT NOT NOW.

Anthem 83.

I SHALL SEE HIM, BUT NOT NOW.

Anthem 83.

I SHALL SEE HIM, BUT NOT NOW.

Anthem 83.

SHALL SEE HIM, BUT NOT NOW.

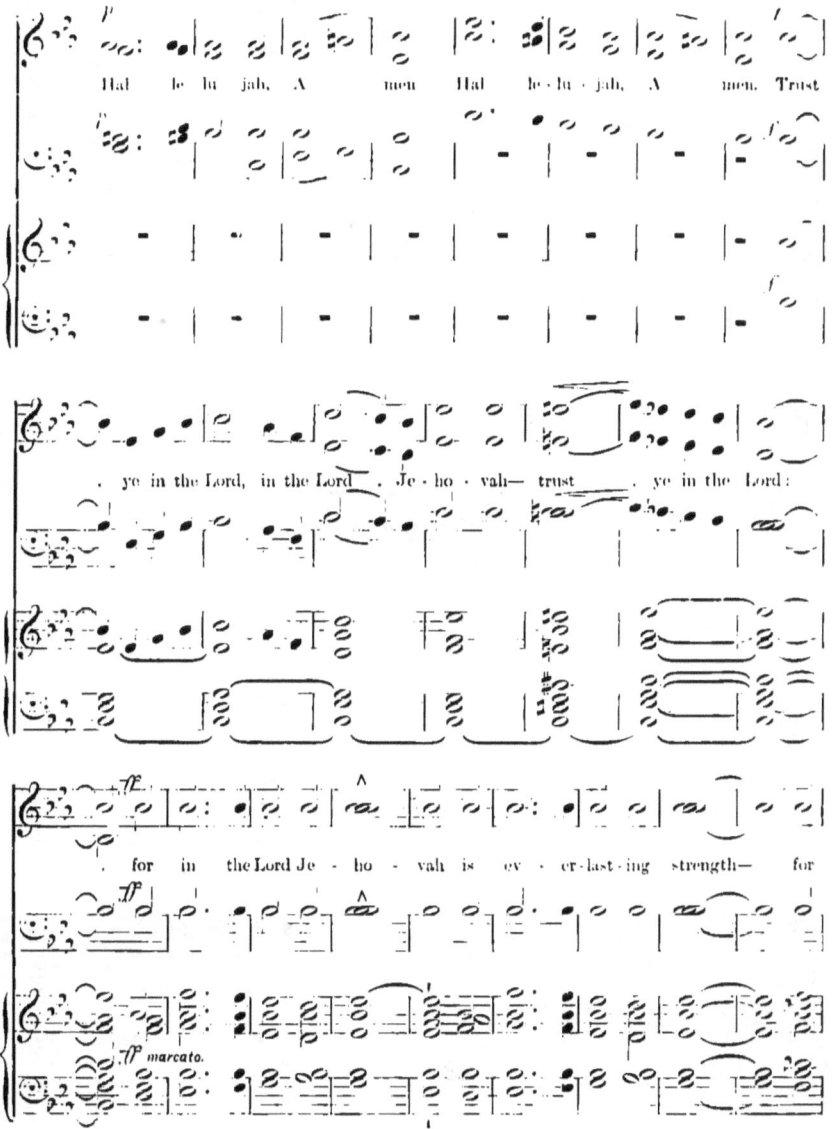

Anthem 83.

I SHALL SEE HIM, BUT NOT NOW.

198

Anthem 84.

BLESSED BE THOU, LORD GOD

* This Anthem may be abbreviated by omitting those portions between the asterisks [✻   ✻].

Anthem 84.

BLESSED BE THOU, LORD GOD.

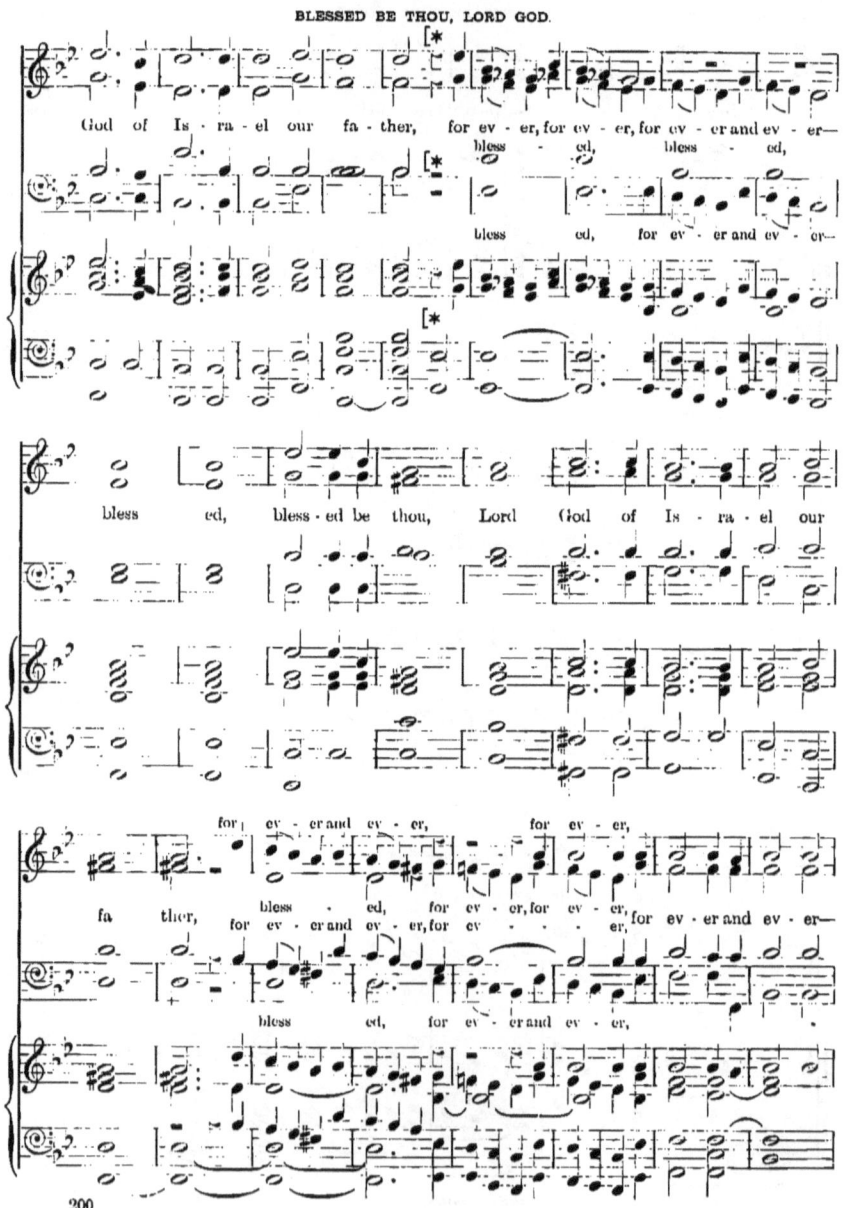

Anthem 84.
BLESSED BE THOU, LORD GOD

Anthem 84.

BLESSED BE THOU, LORD GOD.

and the vic-to-ry, and the maj-es-ty, the vic-to-ry and maj-es-ty— thine, O Lord, thine, O Lord, is the great-ness, and the pow'r, is the great-ness, and the pow'r, and the glo-ry, and the vic-to-ry, and the maj-es-ty, the maj-es-ty: for

Anthem 84.

BLESSED BE THOU, LORD GOD.

all that is in the heav'n, in the heav'n and the earth are thine;
for all that is

for all that is

thine is the king-dom, thine is the king-dom, O Lord, and thou art ex-alt-ed as

head o-ver all, as head o-ver all, as head, as head o-ver all.
o-ver,

Anthem 84.

BLESSED BE THOU, LORD GOD

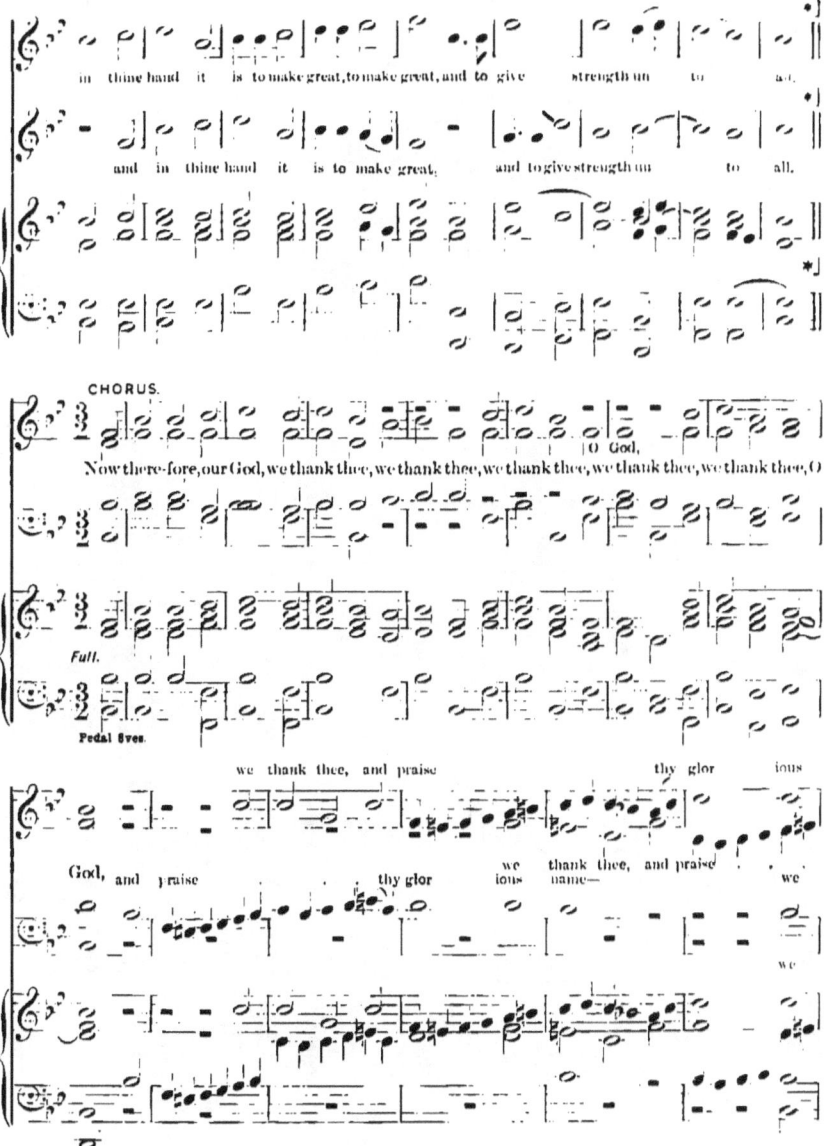

Anthem 84.
BLESSED BE THOU, LORD GOD.

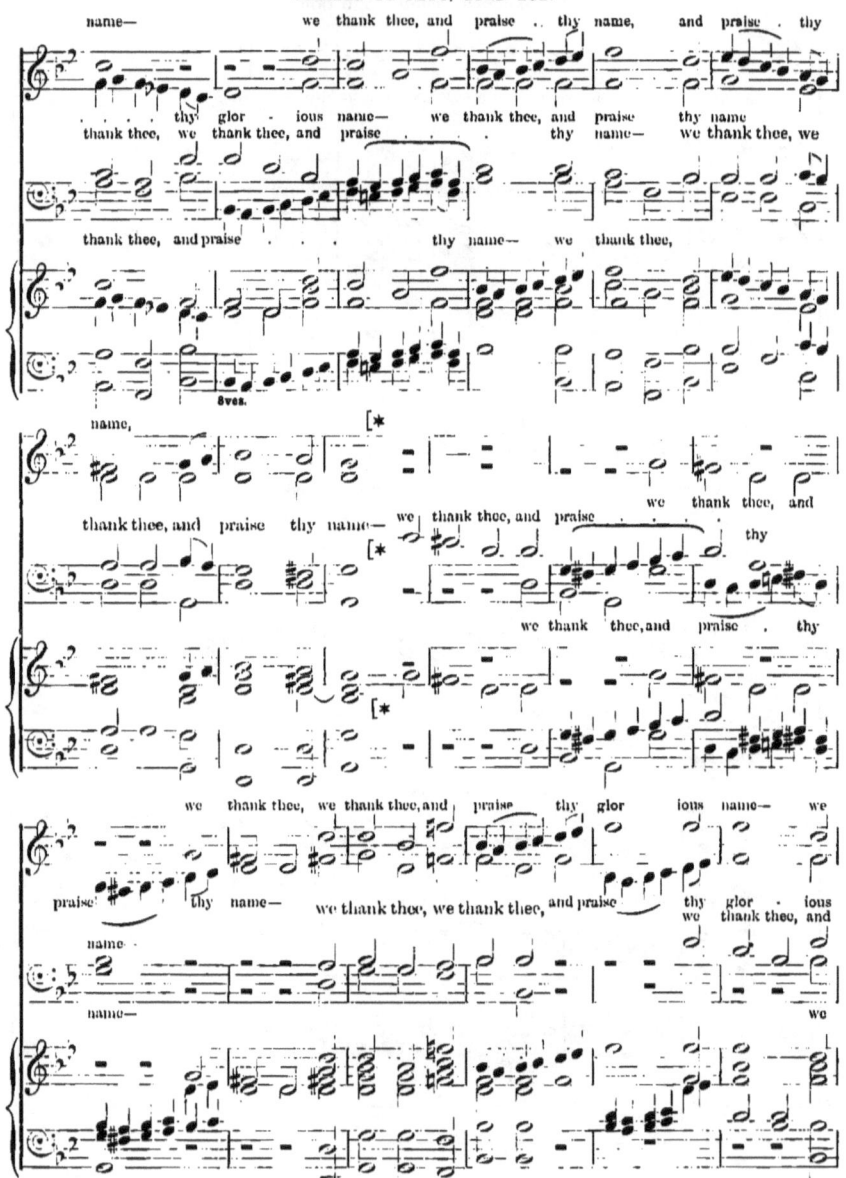

Anthem 84.
BLESSED BE THOU, LORD GOD.

Anthem 85.

I WILL SING OF THE LORD.

Ty. xiii. 6.

Mozart. *Adapted to English words by A. L. Peace, Mus. D.*

Moderato.

TREBLE.

I . . will sing, . . will sing of the Lord—

Anthem 85.

I WILL SING OF THE LORD

Anthem 85.

I WILL SING OF THE LORD.

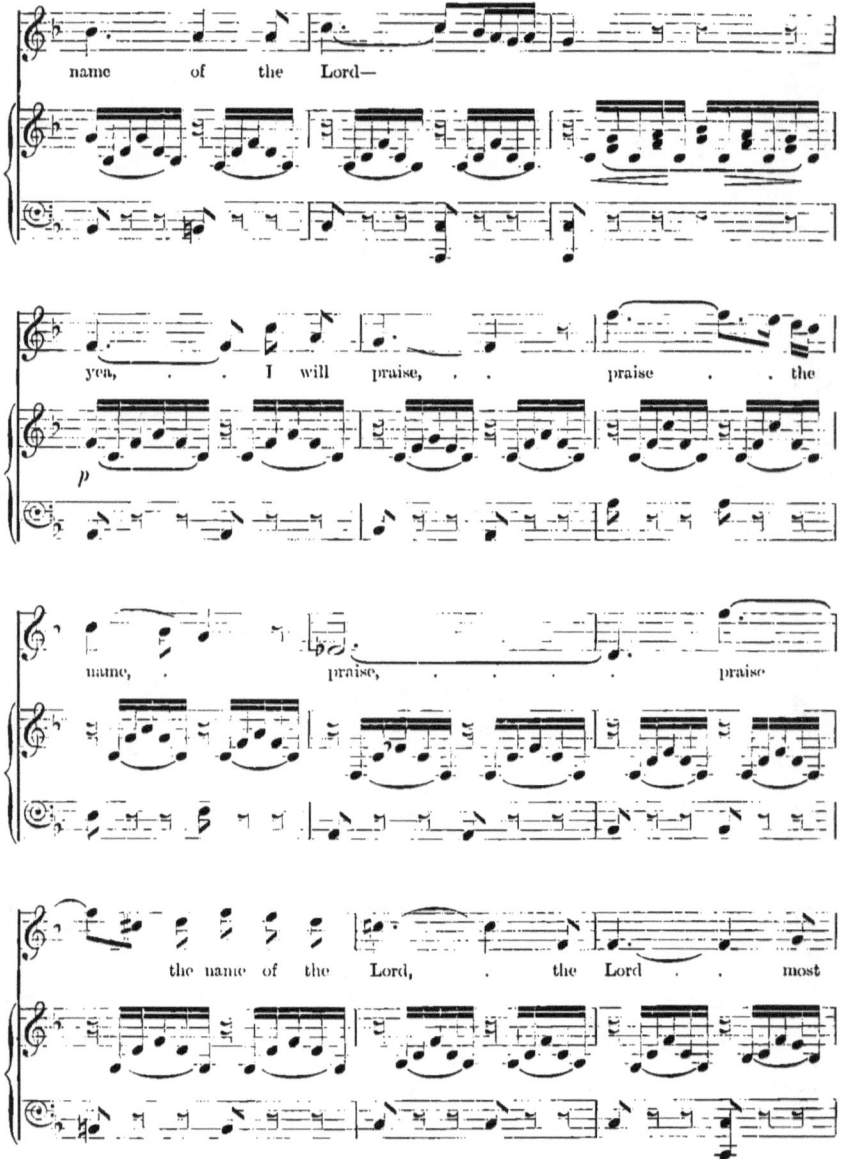

Anthem 85.
I WILL SING OF THE LORD.

Anthem 85.

I WILL SING OF THE LORD.

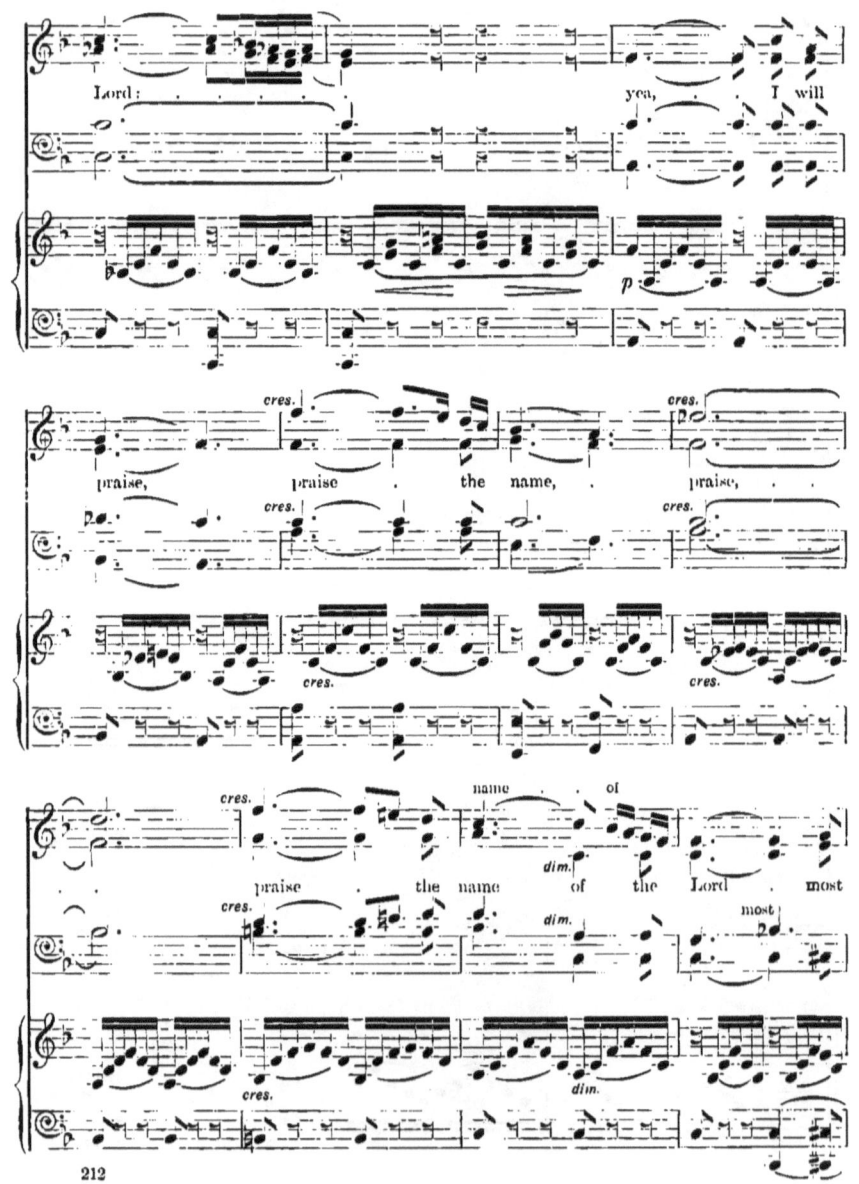

Anthem 85.
I WILL SING OF THE LORD

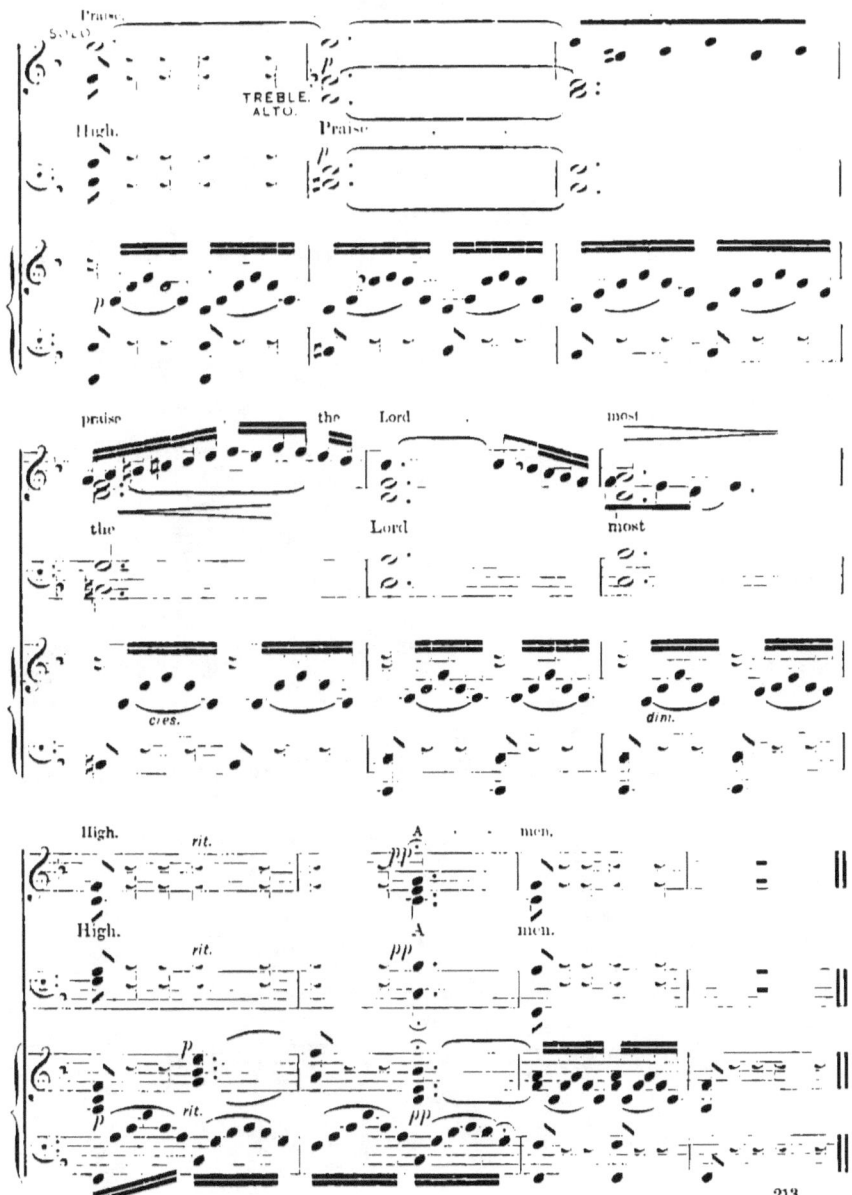

213

Anthem 86.

THE LORD IS MY SHEPHERD.

Ps. xxiii. 1-6.   *Henry Smart.*

Anthem 86.

THE LORD IS MY SHEPHERD.

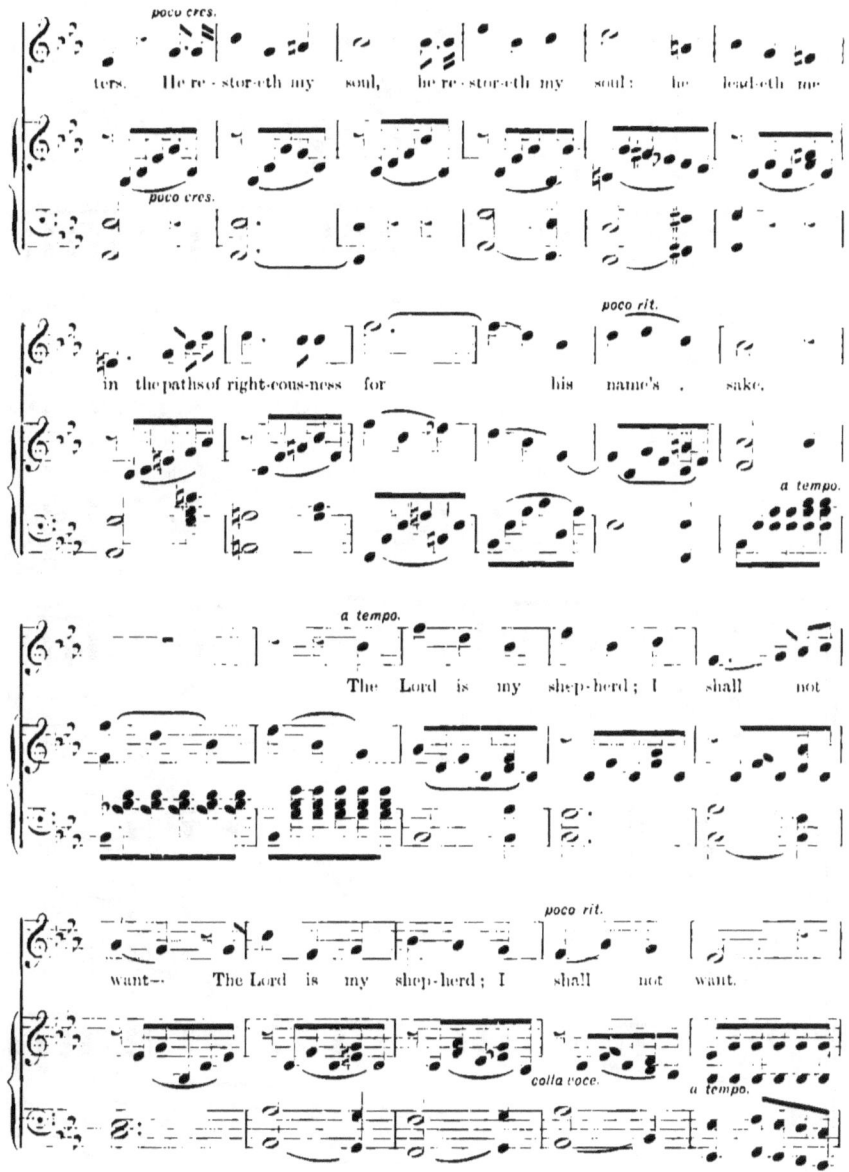

Anthem 86.
THE LORD IS MY SHEPHERD.

Anthem 86.
THE LORD IS MY SHEPHERD

Anthem 86.

THE LORD IS MY SHEPHERD.

Anthem 86.

THE LORD IS MY SHEPHERD

Anthem 86.
THE LORD IS MY SHEPHERD.

Anthem 86.
THE LORD IS MY SHEPHERD

Anthem 87.

O LOVE THE LORD.

* The small notes form the tenor part.

Anthem 87.

O LOVE THE LORD.

Anthem 87.

O LOVE THE LORD.

Anthem 88.

Ps. xxxiv. 1-3. I WILL ALWAY GIVE THANKS. *J. Clarke-Whitfeld, Mus. D.*

I will al-way give thanks un-to the Lord, will al-way give thanks un-to the Lord; his praise shall be ev-er in my mouth— his praise shall be ev-er in my mouth— his praise shall be ev-er

Anthem 88.

I WILL ALWAY GIVE THANKS

Anthem 88.

I WILL ALWAY GIVE THANKS.

Anthem 88.

I WILL ALWAY GIVE THANKS

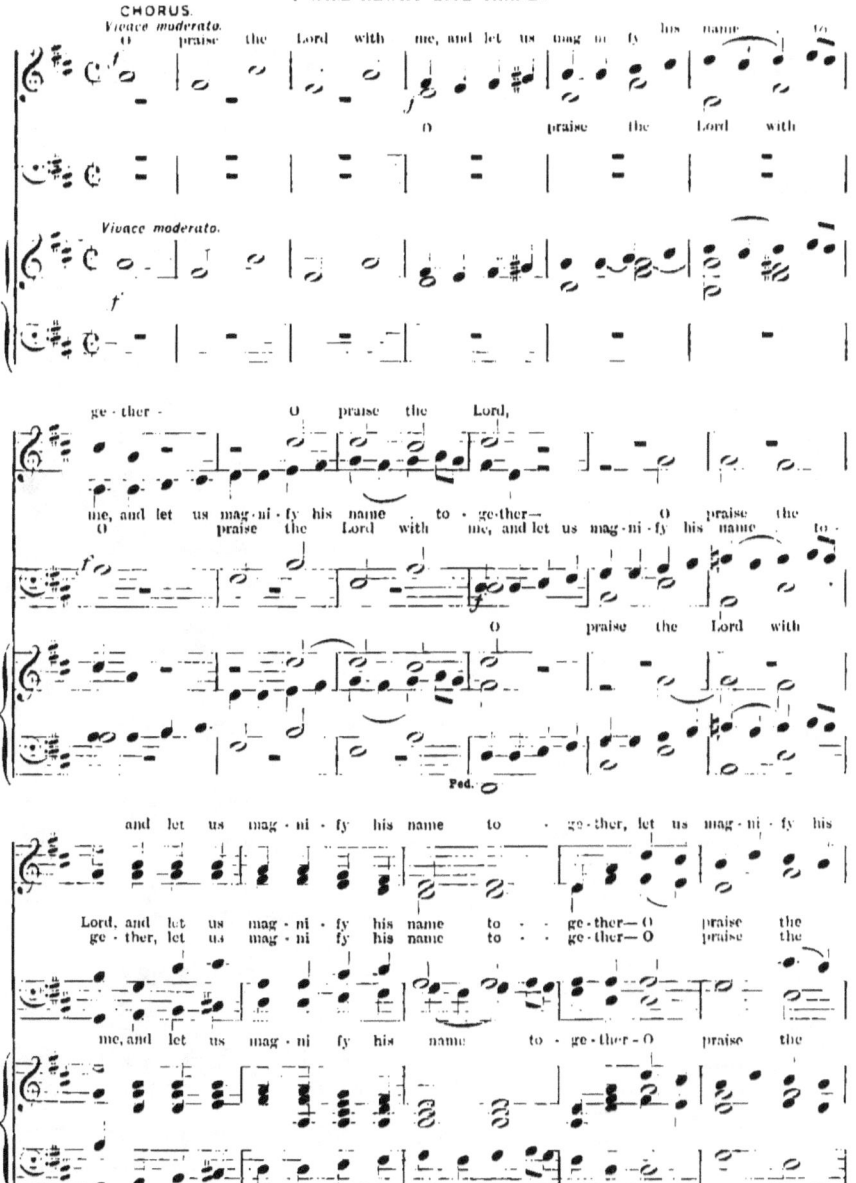

Anthem 88.
I WILL ALWAY GIVE THANKS.

230

Anthem 88.
I WILL ALWAY GIVE THANKS

Anthem 89.

HEAR MY PRAYER, O GOD.

Anthem 89.

HEAR MY PRAYER, O GOD.

Anthem 89.

HEAR MY PRAYER, O GOD

Anthem 89.

HEAR MY PRAYER, O GOD.

Anthem 89.

HEAR MY PRAYER, O GOD.

Anthem 89.
HEAR MY PRAYER, O GOD.

Anthem 89.

HEAR MY PRAYER, O GOD.

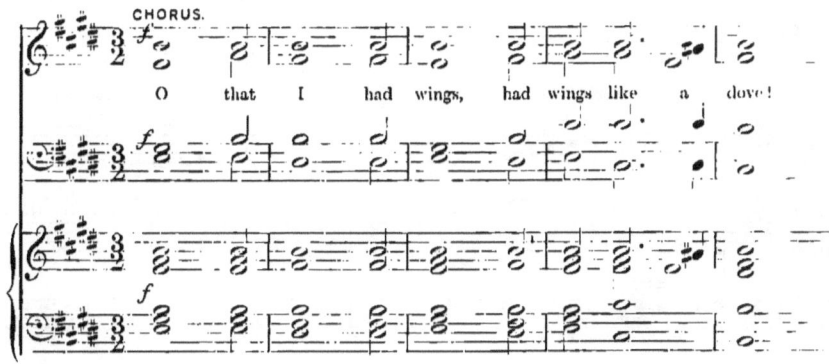

Anthem 89.

HEAR MY PRAYER, O GOD.

240

Anthem 89.
HEAR MY PRAYER, O GOD.

Anthem 90.
MY SOUL TRULY WAITETH STILL UPON GOD

Anthem 90.

MY SOUL TRULY WAITETH STILL UPON GOD.

Anthem 90.

MY SOUL TRULY WAITETH STILL UPON GOD.

245

Anthem 90.

MY SOUL TRULY WAITETH STILL UPON GOD.

Anthem 90.

MY SOUL TRULY WAITETH STILL UPON GOD

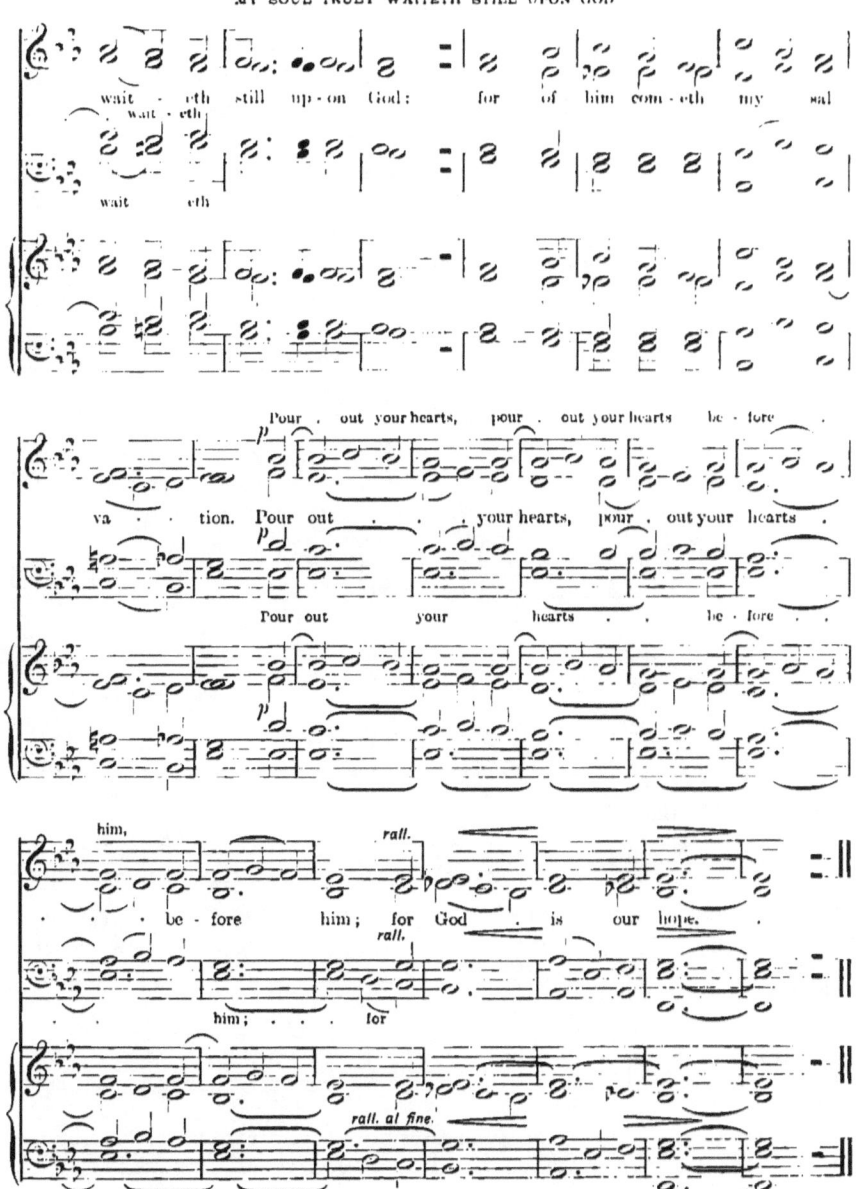

Anthem 91.

GOD BE MERCIFUL UNTO US.

Ps. lxvii. Thomas Bridgewater.

248

Anthem 91.

GOD BE MERCIFUL UNTO US

Anthem 91.

GOD BE MERCIFUL UNTO US

Anthem 91.
GOD BE MERCIFUL UNTO US.

Anthem 92.

Ps. lxvii. 5, 6, 1.   LET THE PEOPLE PRAISE THEE, O GOD.   Sir Michael Costa.

254

Anthem 92.
LET THE PEOPLE PRAISE THEE, O GOD.

Anthem 93.

Ps lxxxiv 4, 5, 12. BLESSED ARE THEY THAT DWELL IN THY HOUSE. *Arthur H. Marchant Mus.B.*

Anthem 93.

BLESSED ARE THEY THAT DWELL IN THY HOUSE.

Anthem 93.

BLESSED ARE THEY THAT DWELL IN THY HOUSE

Anthem 93.

BLESSED ARE THEY THAT DWELL IN THY HOUSE.

260

Anthem 93.

BLESSED ARE THEY THAT DWELL IN THY HOUSE

Anthem 94.

A DAY IN THY COURTS.

Anthem 94.
A DAY IN THY COURTS.

Anthem 94.
A DAY IN THY COURTS.

Anthem 94.

A DAY IN THY COURTS.

Anthem 94.

A DAY IN THY COURTS.

Anthem 94.

A DAY IN THY COURTS.

Anthem 94.
A DAY IN THY COURTS.

Anthem 95.

Ps. lxxxviii. 1-3, 7; lxxxvi. 15, 16.   O LORD GOD OF MY SALVATION.   J. Clarke-Whitfeld, Mus. D.

Anthem 95.
O LORD GOD OF MY SALVATION.

Anthem 95.

O LORD GOD OF MY SALVATION.

Anthem 95.

O LORD GOD OF MY SALVATION.

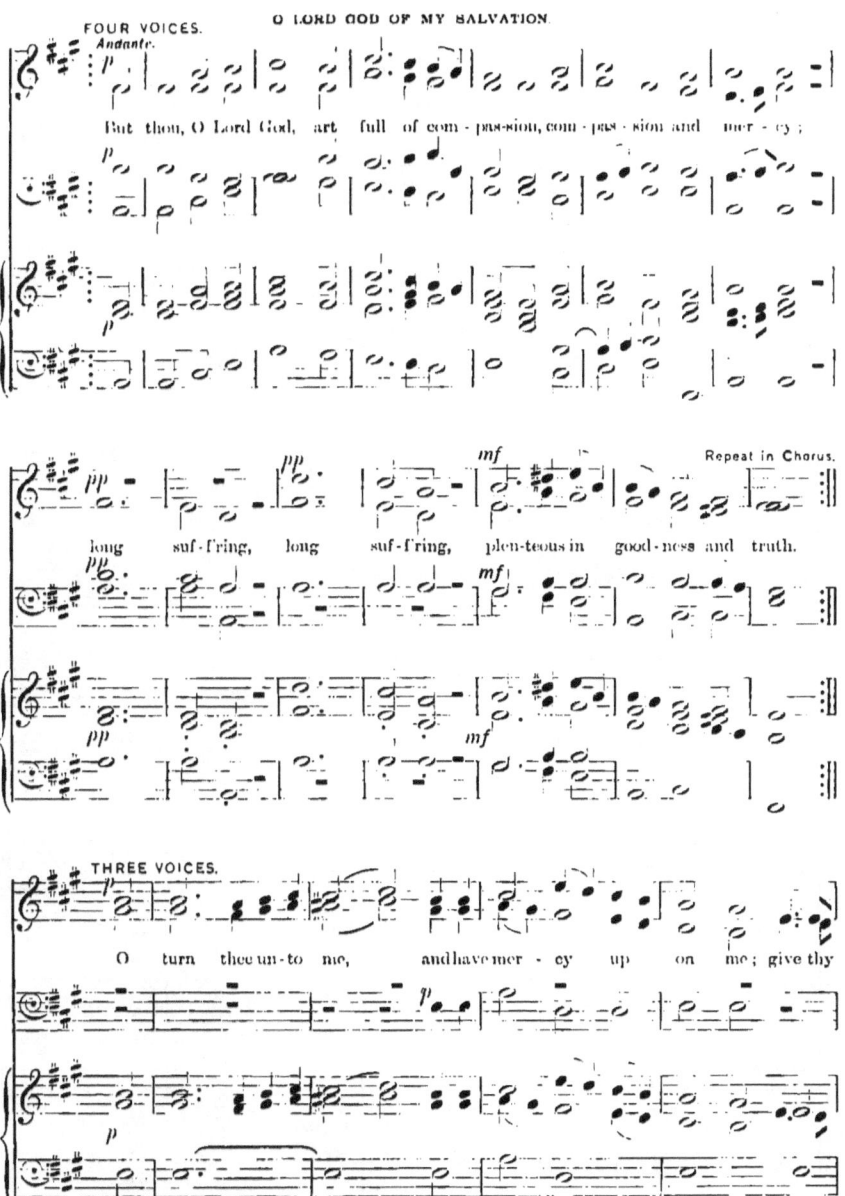

Anthem 96.

TURN THEE AGAIN, O LORD

Anthem 96.

TURN THEE AGAIN, O LORD.

Anthem 96.
TURN THEE AGAIN, O LORD.

Anthem 96.
TURN THEE AGAIN, O LORD.

Anthem 97.

O BE JOYFUL IN THE LORD.

Anthem 97.

O BE JOYFUL IN THE LORD.

Anthem 97.

O BE JOYFUL IN THE LORD.

Anthem 97.

O BE JOYFUL IN THE LORD.

Anthem 98.

Anthem 98.

LORD, HEAR MY PRAYER.

284

Anthem 98.

LORD, HEAR MY PRAYER.

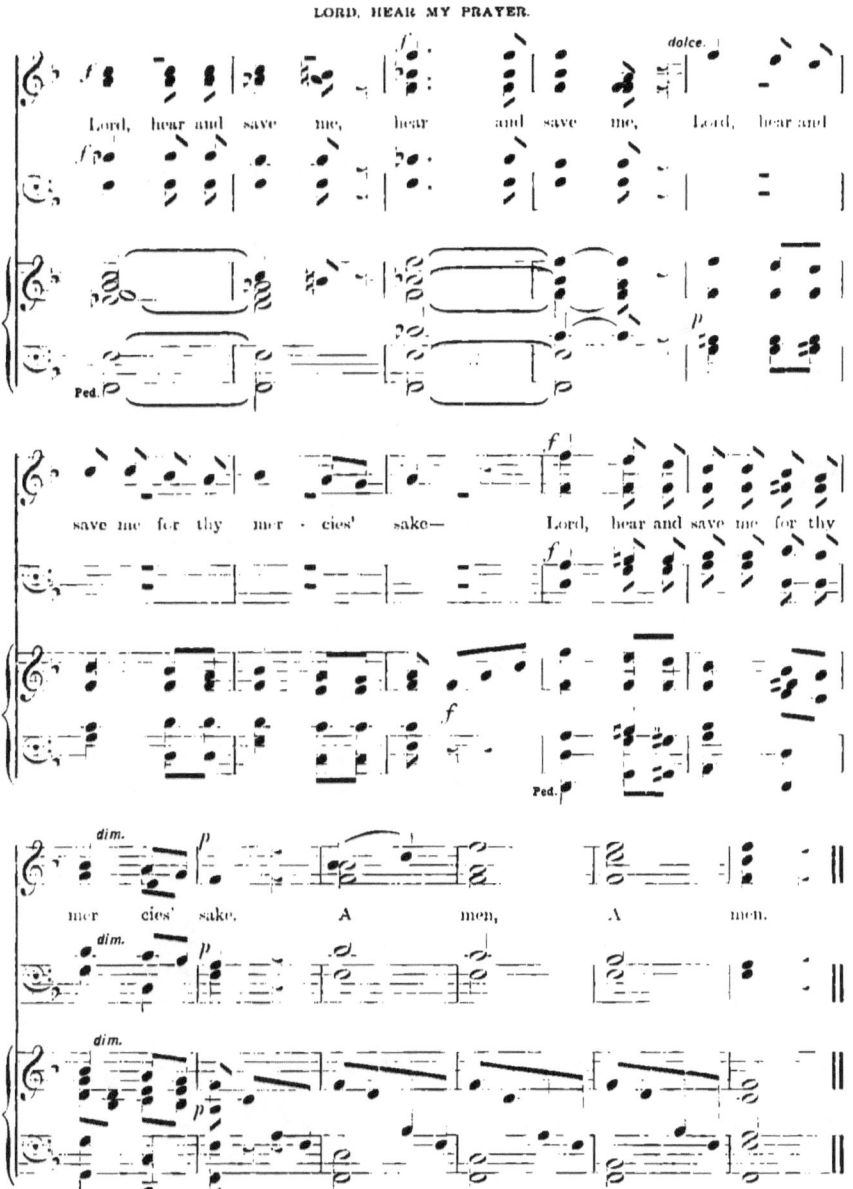

Anthem 99.

Anthem 99.
THE LORD IS FULL OF COMPASSION

Anthem 99.
THE LORD IS FULL OF COMPASSION.

Anthem 99.

THE LORD IS FULL OF COMPASSION

Anthem 100.

THE LORD IS FULL OF COMPASSION.

Anthem 100.

THE LORD IS FULL OF COMPASSION.

Anthem 100.
THE LORD IS FULL OF COMPASSION

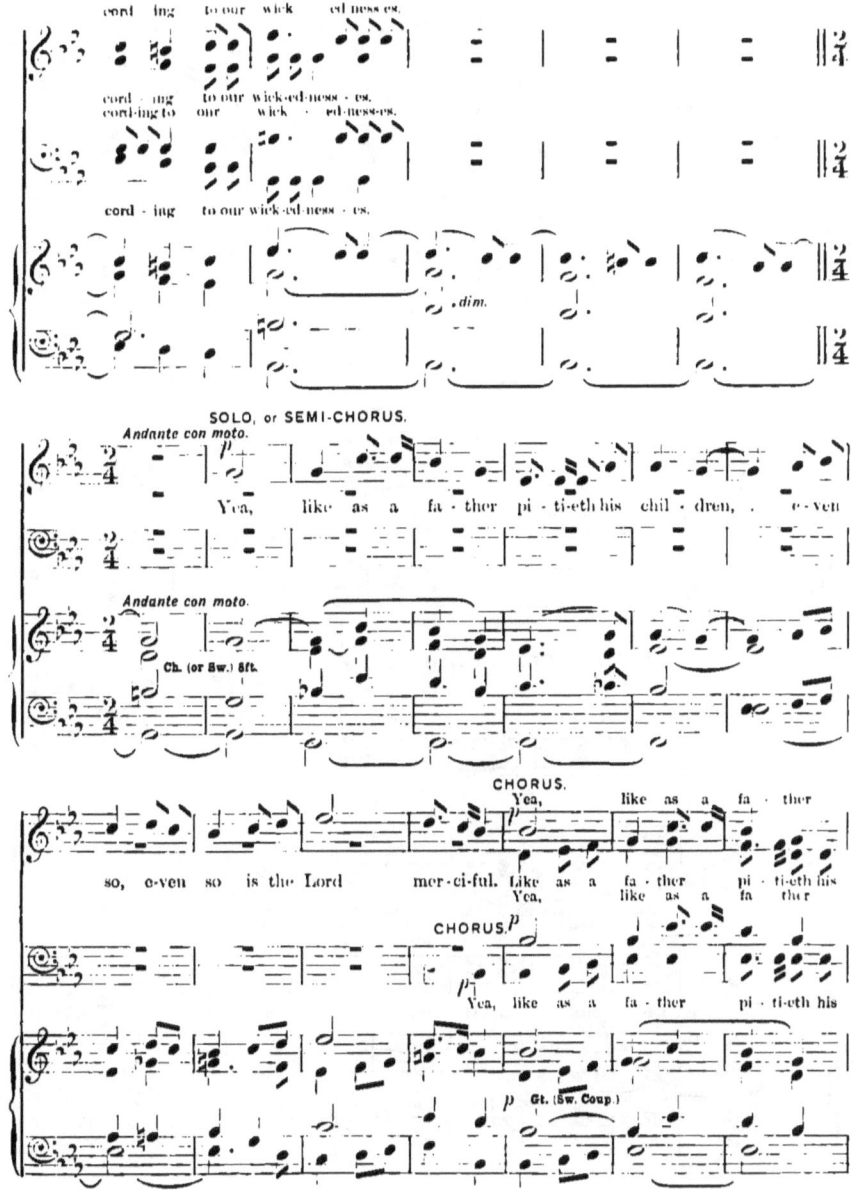

Anthem 100.
THE LORD IS FULL OF COMPASSION.

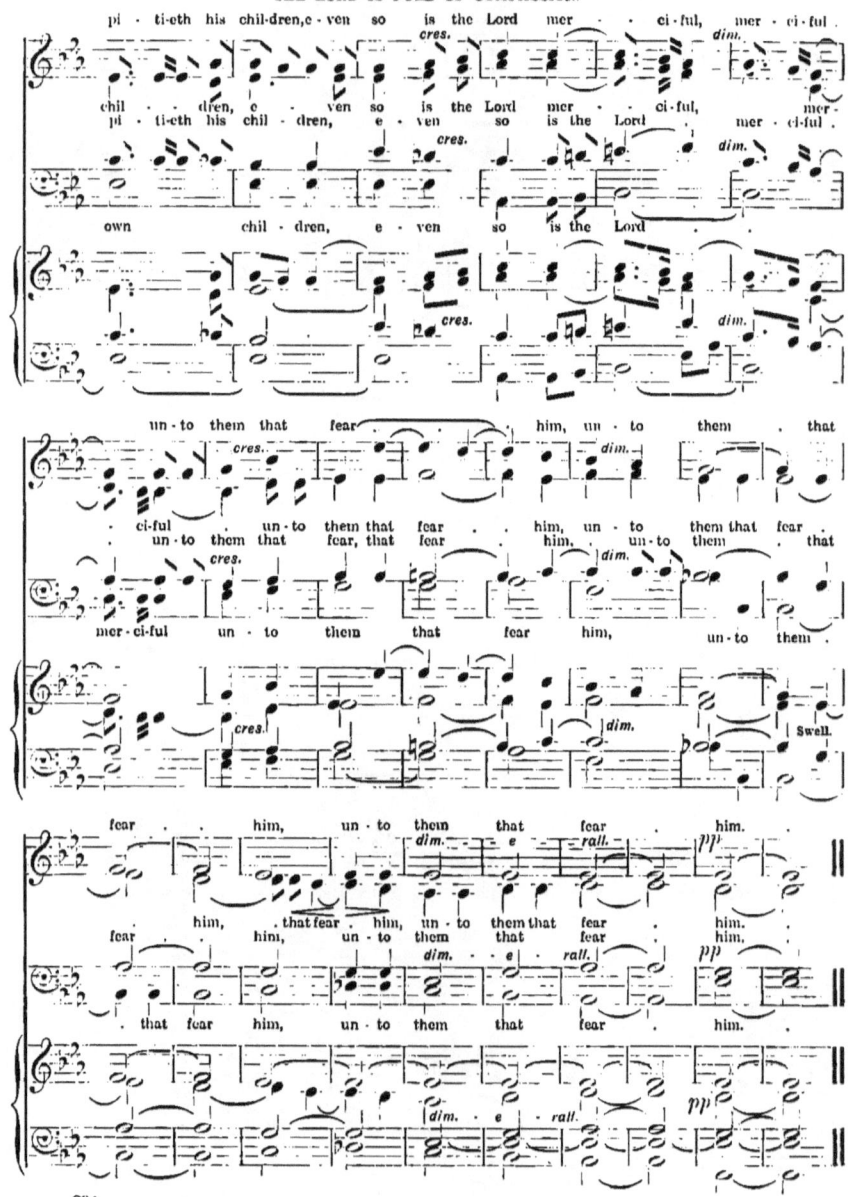

Anthem 101.

Ps. cxii. 1 3. BLESSED IS THE MAN THAT FEARETH THE LORD. *J. Clarke-Whitfeld, Mus. D.*

Anthem 101.

BLESSED IS THE MAN THAT FEARETH THE LORD.

296

Anthem 101.

BLESSED IS THE MAN THAT FEARETH THE LORD.

Anthem 101.

BLESSED IS THE MAN THAT FEARETH THE LORD

Anthem 102.

Ps. cxvii.   O PRAISE THE LORD, ALL YE NATIONS.   Sir H. S. Oakeley, Mus. D.

O praise the Lord, all ye nations; praise him, all ye people praise

.. the Lord, all ye nations; praise him, all ye people.

Slower and softer.
For his merciful kindness is great toward us, his

Slower and softer.
Choir Organ.

Manuale solamente.   Ped.

301

Anthem 102.

O PRAISE THE LORD, ALL YE NATIONS.

Anthem 102.
O PRAISE THE LORD, ALL YE NATIONS.

Anthem 102.

O PRAISE THE LORD, ALL YE NATIONS.

Anthem 102.
O PRAISE THE LORD, ALL YE NATIONS.

Anthem 103.

Ps. cxxx. 1-4. OUT OF THE DEEP HAVE I CALLED UNTO THEE. Mozart.

Anthem 103.
OUT OF THE DEEP HAVE I CALLED UNTO THEE

Anthem 103.

OUT OF THE DEEP HAVE I CALLED UNTO THEE.

Anthem 104.

Isa. lx. 19, 20. THE SUN SHALL BE NO MORE THY LIGHT BY DAY. A. L. Peace, Mus. D.

Anthem 104.

THE SUN SHALL BE NO MORE THY LIGHT BY DAY.

Anthem 104.

THE SUN SHALL BE NO MORE THY LIGHT BY DAY.

312

Anthem 105.

Anthem 105.
LET US NOW FEAR THE LORD.

Anthem 105.
LET US NOW FEAR THE LORD

Anthem 105.
LET US NOW FEAR THE LORD.

Anthem 106.

Anthem 106.

COME, AND LET US GO UP.

Anthem 106.
COME, AND LET US GO UP

Anthem 106.
COME, AND LET US GO UP.

Anthem 106.
COME, AND LET US GO UP.

Anthem 106.
COME, AND LET US GO UP.

322

Anthem 106.

COME, AND LET US GO UP

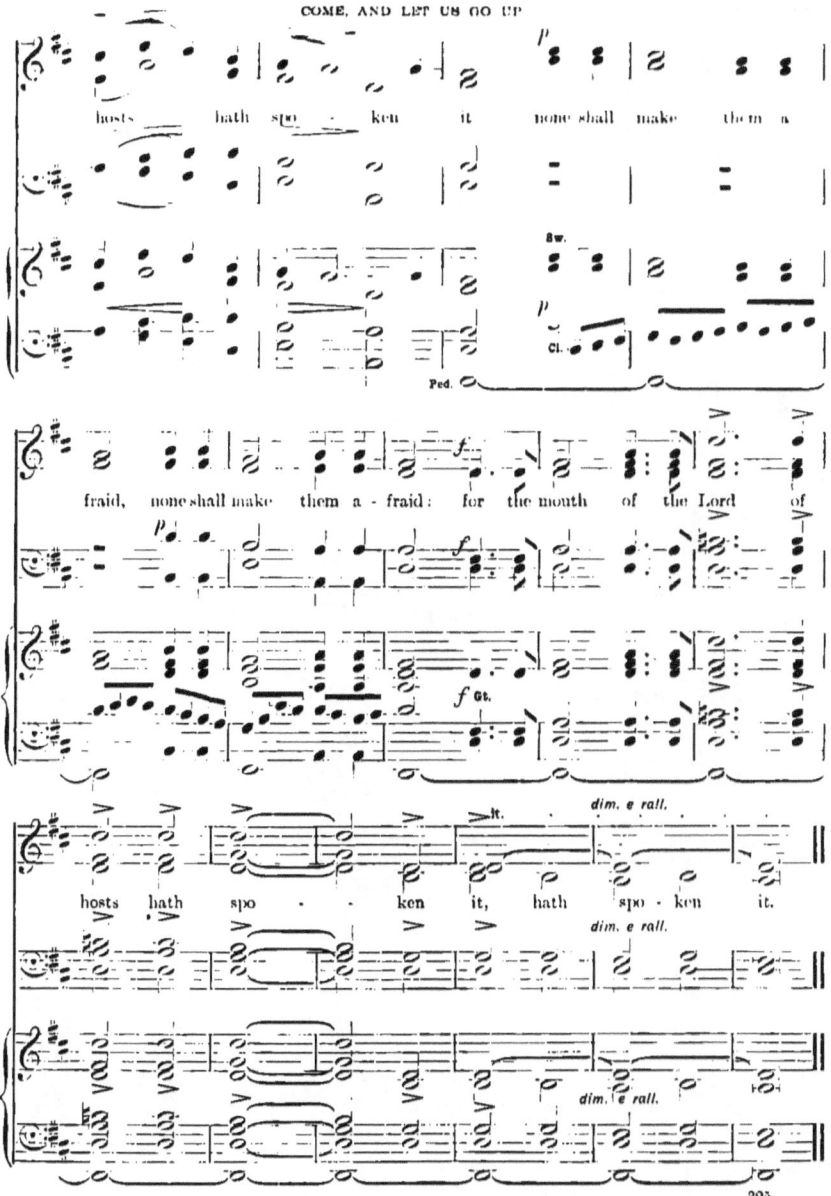

Anthem 107.

HE THAT SHALL ENDURE TO THE END

Anthem 107.
HE THAT SHALL ENDURE TO THE END.

Anthem 108.

MY SOUL DOTH MAGNIFY THE LORD.

Luke I. 46-55. Benjamin Cooke, Mus. D.

Anthem 108.
MY SOUL DOTH MAGNIFY THE LORD.

Anthem 108.

MY SOUL DOTH MAGNIFY THE LORD.

Anthem 108.
MY SOUL DOTH MAGNIFY THE LORD.

Anthem 108.
MY SOUL DOTH MAGNIFY THE LORD

Anthem 108.

MY SOUL DOTH MAGNIFY THE LORD.

* The small note forms the alto part.

Anthem 108.

MY SOUL DOTH MAGNIFY THE LORD.

Anthem 109.
MY SOUL DOTH MAGNIFY THE LORD.

Anthem 109.

MY SOUL DOTH MAGNIFY THE LORD.

Anthem 109.

MY SOUL DOTH MAGNIFY THE LORD

Anthem 109.
MY SOUL DOTH MAGNIFY THE LORD.

Anthem 109.
MY SOUL DOTH MAGNIFY THE LORD

Anthem 109.

MY SOUL DOTH MAGNIFY THE LORD.

Anthem 110.

Anthem 110.

BLESSED BE THE LORD GOD OF ISRAEL.

Anthem 110.
BLESSED BE THE LORD GOD OF ISRAEL.

Anthem 110.
BLESSED BE THE LORD GOD OF ISRAEL.

Anthem 110
BLESSED BE THE LORD GOD OF ISRAEL.

347

Anthem 110.

BLESSED BE THE LORD GOD OF ISRAEL.

Anthem 110.

BLESSED BE THE LORD GOD OF ISRAEL.

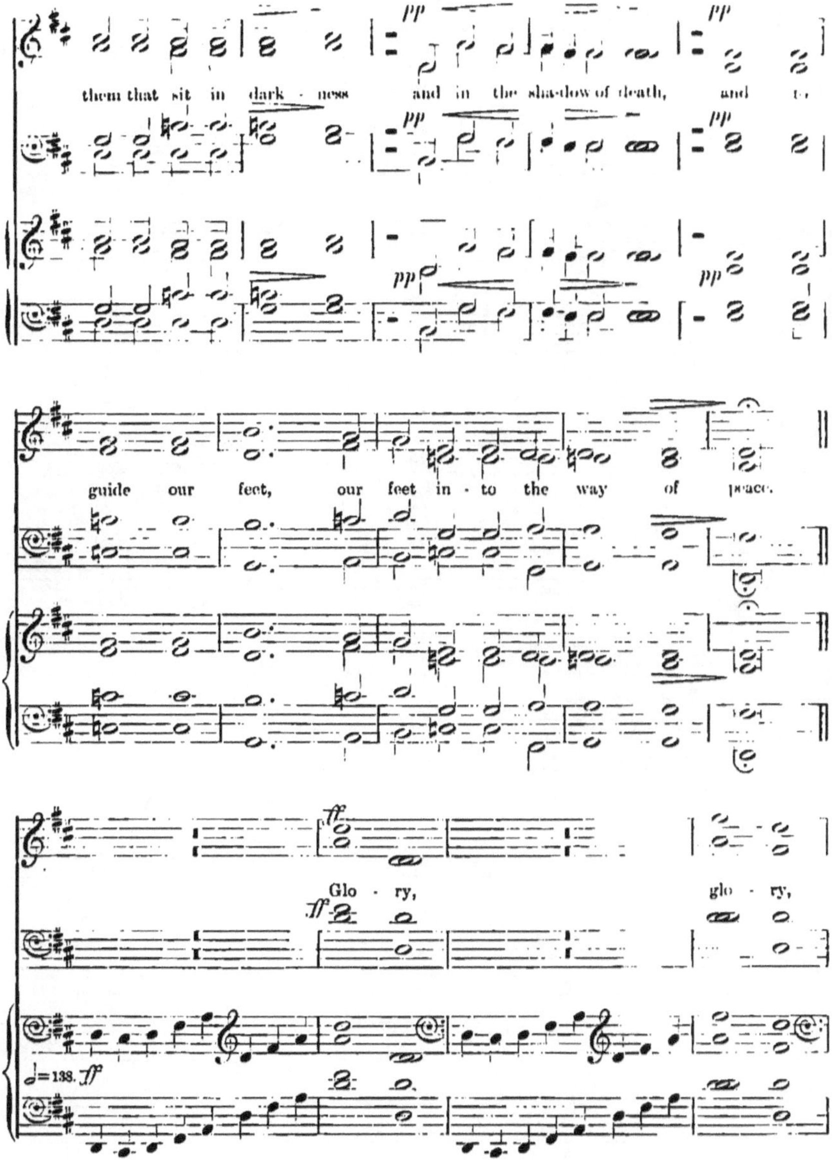

them that sit in dark - ness and in the sha-dow of death, and to

guide our feet, our feet in-to the way of peace.

Glo - ry, glo - ry,

♩=138. *ff*

Anthem 110.

BLESSED BE THE LORD GOD OF ISRAEL.

Anthem 110.

BLESSED BE THE LORD GOD OF ISRAEL

351

Anthem 110.
BLESSED BE THE LORD GOD OF ISRAEL.

Anthem 111.

Anthem 111.
LET US NOW GO EVEN UNTO BETHLEHEM.

Anthem 111.

LET US NOW GO EVEN UNTO BETHLEHEM

Anthem 111.
LET US NOW GO EVEN UNTO BETHLEHEM.

356

Anthem 111.

LET US NOW GO EVEN UNTO BETHLEHEM

Anthem 111.
LET US NOW GO EVEN UNTO BETHLEHEM.

Anthem 112.

LORD, NOW LETTEST THOU

Anthem 112.
LORD, NOW LETTEST THOU.

Anthem 112.

LORD, NOW LETTEST THOU.

Anthem 112.

LORD, NOW LETTEST THOU.

Anthem 112.

LORD, NOW LETTEST THOU.

Anthem 113.

NOW WE ARE AMBASSADORS

Anthem 113.

HOW LOVELY ARE THE MESSENGERS

Anthem 113.

HOW LOVELY ARE THE MESSENGERS.

Anthem 113.
HOW LOVELY ARE THE MESSENGERS

Anthem 113.
HOW LOVELY ARE THE MESSENGERS.

Anthem 113.

HOW LOVELY ARE THE MESSENGERS

Anthem 113.
HOW LOVELY ARE THE MESSENGERS.

Anthem 114.

BLESSING, HONOUR, GLORY, AND POWER

Anthem 114.

BLESSING, HONOUR, GLORY, AND POWER.

Anthem 114.
BLESSING, HONOUR, GLORY, AND POWER

Anthem 114.
BLESSING, HONOUR, GLORY, AND POWER.

Anthem 114.

BLESSING, HONOUR, GLORY, AND POWER

Anthem 114.

BLESSING, HONOUR, GLORY, AND POWER.

378

Anthem 114.
BLESSING, HONOUR, GLORY, AND POWER

Anthem 115.

LORD, HAVE MERCY UPON US.

* *The small notes form the chorus alto part.*

Anthem 115.
LORD, HAVE MERCY UPON US

The small notes form the chorus alto part.

Anthem 115.
LORD, HAVE MERCY UPON US.

Anthem 116.
O LORD, WE PRAY THEE.

Anthem 116.
O LORD, WE PRAY THEE.

386

Anthem 116.

O LORD, WE PRAY THEE.

Anthem 116.
O LORD, WE PRAY THEE.

Anthem 116.

O LORD, WE PRAY THEE.

Anthem 117.

HOLY, HOLY, HOLY IS GOD OUR LORD. — *Spohr.*

Anthem 117.

HOLY, HOLY, HOLY IS GOD OUR LORD.

Anthem 118.

Anthem 118.

HOLY ART THOU, O LORD OF HOSTS

Anthem 119.

Anthem 119.

WE PRAISE THEE, O GOD.

Anthem 119.

WE PRAISE THEE, O GOD.

Anthem 119.

WE PRAISE THEE, O GOD.

Anthem 119.
WE PRAISE THEE, O GOD.

Anthem 119.

WE PRAISE THEE, O GOD.

Anthem 119.

WE PRAISE THEE, O GOD.

400

Anthem 119.

WE PRAISE THEE, O GOD

Anthem 119.

WE PRAISE THEE, O GOD.

Anthem 120.

THY MEMORY, O JESUS SWEET.

Anthem 120.
THY MEMORY, O JESUS SWEET.

get their grief; Who seek thee know their darkness brief. Who find, ah! rap-ture past be-lief. Je - sus, the heart's de- li-cious Balm, Our Life and Light in storm and calm; Je - sus, the heart's de - li-cious Balm, Our Life and Light in

Anthem 120.
THY MEMORY, O JESUS SWEET.

Anthem 120.
THY MEMORY, O JESUS SWEET

Anthem 120.
THY MEMORY, O JESUS SWEET.

THE SCOTTISH ANTHEM BOOK.

WORDS OF ANTHEMS.*

Anthem 121.

Rev. Sir F. A. Gore Ouseley, Bart., Mus. D.

Num. xxiv. 5. How goodly are thy tents, O Jacob, and thy tabernacles, O Israel!

6. As the valleys are they spread forth, as gardens by the river's side.

Anthem 122.

S. S. Wesley, Mus. D.

1 Kings viii. 28. O Lord my God, hear thou the prayer thy servant prayeth; have thou respect unto his prayer.

30. Hear thou in heaven thy dwelling-place: and when thou hearest, Lord, forgive.

Anthem 123.

Henry Gadsby.

Ps. iv. 8. I will lay me down in peace, and take my rest: for it is thou, Lord, only that makest me dwell in safety.

Anthem 124.

A. C. Mackenzie, Mus. D.

Ps. iv. 8. I will lay me down in peace, and take my rest: for it is thou, Lord, only that makest me dwell in safety. Amen.

Anthem 125.

Sir Robert P. Stewart, Mus. D.

Ps. xi. 1. In the Lord put I my trust: how say ye then to my soul that she should flee as a bird unto the hill?

2. For, lo, the ungodly bend their bow, and make ready their arrows within the quiver, that they may privily shoot at them that are true of heart.

4. The Lord is in his holy temple, the Lord's seat is in heaven: his eyes consider the poor, and his eyelids try the children of men.

6. Upon the ungodly he shall rain snares, fire, storm and tempest: this shall be their portion to drink.

7. For the righteous Lord loveth righteousness; his countenance will behold the thing that is just.

Anthem 126.

Mendelssohn.

Ps. xiii.

1. Lord, how long wilt thou forget me,
    While in lonely grief I mourn?
    And how long thy face be hiding—
    Wilt thou nevermore return?
2. Lord, how long must I take counsel,
    Having sorrow in my heart?
    Foes relentless rise against me,
    And no helper take my part?

Anthem 127.

J. Varley Roberts, Mus. D.

Ps. xv. 1. Lord, who shall dwell in thy tabernacle? or who shall rest upon thy holy hill?

2. Even he that leadeth an uncorrupt life, even he that doeth the thing which is right, and speaketh the truth from his heart.

3. He that hath used no deceit in his tongue, nor done evil to his neighbour, and hath not slandered his neighbour.

4. He that setteth not by himself, but is

---

* Music to be had from the Publishers of the several Anthems. See Index, pp. 423, 424.

lowly in his own eyes; and maketh much of them that fear the Lord. He that sweareth unto his neighbour, and disappointeth him not, though it were to his own hindrance.

5. He that hath not given his money upon usury, nor taken reward against the innocent. Whoso doeth these things shall never fall.

Anthem 128.
J. L. Hopkins, Mus. D.

Ps. xxiv. 7. LIFT up your heads, O ye gates; and be ye lift up, ye everlasting doors; and the King of glory shall come in.

8. Who is the King of glory? The Lord strong and mighty, the Lord mighty in battle.

10. The Lord of hosts, he is the King of glory.

Anthem 129.
Vincent Novello.

Ps. xxv. 6. CALL to remembrance thy tender mercies, which have been ever of old.

Ps. vi. 4. Turn thee, O Lord, and deliver my soul: O save me for thy mercies' sake. Amen.

Anthem 130.
Rev. Sir F. A. Gore Ouseley, Bart., Mus. D.

Ps. xxx. 10. HEAR, O Lord, and have mercy upon me: Lord, be thou my helper.

11. Thou hast turned my heaviness into joy: thou hast put off my sackcloth, and girded me with gladness;

12. Therefore shall every good man sing of thy praise without ceasing. O my God, I will give thanks to thee for ever. Amen.

Anthem 131.
J. Baptiste Calkin.

Ps. xxxvii. 37. KEEP innocency, and take heed unto the thing that is right: for that shall bring a man peace at the last.

38. As for the transgressors, they shall perish together: and the end of the ungodly is, they shall be rooted out.

39. But the salvation of the righteous cometh of the Lord: who is also their strength in the time of trouble.

40. And the Lord shall stand by them, and save them: he shall deliver them from the ungodly, because they put their trust in him.

Anthem 132.
Mendelssohn.

Ps. xl. 1. I WAITED for the Lord; he inclined unto me, he heard my complaint.

4. O blessed are they that hope and trust in the Lord.

Anthem 133.
Spohr.

Ps. xlii.
1. As pants the hart for cooling streams,
   When heated in the chase;
   So longs my soul, O God, for thee,
   And thy refreshing grace.
2 For thee, my God, the living God,
   My thirsty soul doth pine:
   Oh, when shall I behold thy face,
   Thou Majesty divine?

Anthem 134.
Charles Gounod.

Ps. xliii. 3. SEND out thy light and thy truth: let them lead me; and let them bring me to thy holy hill.

4. O God, then will I go unto thine altar: on the harp we will praise thee, O Lord our God.

5. Why, O soul, art thou sorrowful? and why cast down within me? Still trust the loving-kindness of the God of thy strength: and my tongue yet shall praise him, who hath pleaded my cause.

Ps. xx. 6. Lord, our God, thou wilt save thine anointed; thou wilt hear us from heaven.

7. Though in chariots some put their faith: our trust is in thee.

8. They are brought down and fallen: but the Lord is our helper, we shall not be afraid.

Anthem 135.

Maurice Greene, Mus. D.

Ps. xlvi. 1. GOD is our hope and strength, a very present help in trouble.
2. Therefore we will not fear, though the earth tremble;
3. Though the mountains shake, and the waters rage and swell.
5. For God is in the midst of us; therefore shall we not be moved: God is our hope and refuge; therefore shall we not be moved.
8. Oh, behold the works of the Lord!
9. He maketh wars to cease in all the world.
10. He is exalted among the heathen; he is exalted in the earth.

Anthem 136.

T. Tallis Trimnell, Mus. B.

Ps. xlvii. 1. O CLAP your hands together, all ye people; O sing unto God with the voice of melody.
2. For the Lord is high, and to be feared; he is the great King upon all the earth.

Anthem 137.

J. Baptiste Calkin.

Ps. li. 17. THE sacrifices of God are a broken spirit: a broken heart, and a contrite heart, O God, thou wilt not despise.

Anthem 138.

J. L. Hopkins, Mus. D.

Ps. liv. 1. SAVE me, O God, for thy name's sake, and avenge me in thy strength.
3. For strangers are risen up against me; and tyrants, which have not God before their eyes, seek after my soul.

Anthem 139.

Mendelssohn.

Ps. lv.
1. HEAR my prayer, O God; incline thine ear: Thyself from my petition do not hide.
2. Take heed to me; hear how in prayer I mourn to thee:
Without thee all is dark; I have no guide.
3. The enemy shouteth; the godless come fast:
Iniquity, hatred upon me they cast.
The wicked oppress me: ah, where shall I fly?
Perplexed and bewildered, O God, hear my cry.
4. My heart is sorely pained within my breast, My soul with deadly terror is oppressed.
5. Trembling and fearfulness upon me fall, With horror overwhelmed, Lord, hear me call.
6. Oh for the wings, for the wings of a dove! Far away, far away would I rove;
7. In the wilderness build me a nest,
And remain there for ever at rest.

Anthem 140.

A. L. Peace, Mus. D.

Ps. lvii. 8. AWAKE up, my glory; awake, lute and harp: I myself will awake right early: and I will sing unto thee, O Lord, among the nations.
9. I will give thanks unto thee, O Lord, among the people; and I will sing unto thee among the nations.
10. For the greatness of thy mercy reacheth unto the heavens, and thy truth unto the clouds.
11. Set up thyself, O God, above the heavens; and thy glory above all the earth.

Anthem 141.

W. Hutchins Callcott.

Ps. lxv. 9. THOU visitest the earth, and blessest it: thou makest it very plenteous.
11. Thou crownest the year with thy goodness; and thy clouds drop fatness.
13. The valleys stand so thick with corn, that they laugh and sing.

WORDS OF ANTHEMS.

Anthem 142.
J. Clarke-Whitfeld, Mus. D.

Ps. lxxvi. 1. IN Jewry is God known: his name is great in Israel.
2. At Salem is his tabernacle, and his dwelling in Zion.
3. There brake he the arrows of the bow, the shield, the sword, and the battle.

Anthem 143.
Charles Steggall, Mus. D.

Ps. lxxvii. 1. I WILL cry unto God with my voice, even unto God will I cry with my voice; and he shall hearken unto me.
3. When I am in heaviness, I will think upon God: when my heart is vexed, I will complain.
5. I have considered the days of old, and the years that are past.
6. I commune with my own heart in the night: I search out my spirit.
11. I will remember the works of the Lord; and will call to mind thy wonders of old time.
12. I will also think of all thy works, and my talking shall be of thy doings.

Anthem 144.
J. Clarke-Whitfeld, Mus. D.

Ps. lxxx. 1. HEAR, O thou Shepherd of Israel, thou that leadest Joseph like a sheep; shew thyself also, thou that sittest upon the cherubims.
3. Turn us again, O God; shew the light of thy countenance, and we shall be whole.
4. Lord God of hosts, how long wilt thou be angry with thy people that prayeth?
5. Thou feedest them with the bread of tears; and giv'st us plenteousness of tears to drink.
8. Thou hast brought a vine out of Egypt: thou hast cast out the heathen, and planted it.
10. The hills were covered with the shadow of it, and the boughs thereof were like the goodly cedar trees.
11. She stretched out her branches unto the sea, and her boughs unto the river.

412

12. Why hast thou then broken down her hedge, that all they that go by pluck off her grapes?
14. Turn thee again, thou God of hosts: behold, and visit this vine.
18. And so will we not go back from thee: O let us live, and we shall call upon thy name.

Anthem 145.
Joseph Barnby.

Ps. lxxxiv. 1. O how amiable are thy dwellings, thou Lord of hosts!
2. My soul hath a desire and longing to enter into the courts of the house of the Lord: my heart and my flesh rejoice in the living God.
4. Blessed are they that dwell in thy house: they will be alway praising thee.
Glory be to the Father, and to the Son, and to the Holy Ghost;
As it was in the beginning, is now, and ever shall be, world without end. Amen.

Anthem 146.
T. Mee Pattison.

Ps. lxxxiv. 1. O how amiable are thy dwellings, thou Lord of hosts!
2. My soul hath a desire and longing to enter into the courts of the Lord.
3. Yea, the sparrow hath found her a house, and the swallow a nest, where she may lay her young, even thine altars, O Lord of hosts, my King, and my God.
4. Blessed are they that dwell in thy house: they will be alway praising thee.
5. And blessed is the man whose strength is in thee; and in whose heart are thy ways.

Anthem 147.
William Bird.

Ps. lxxxvi. 1. Bow thine ear, O Lord, and hear: let thine anger cease from us.
ISA. lxiv. 10. Zion, thy Zion is wasted and brought low; Jerusalem is wasted quite, desolate and void.

Anthem 148.

T. Mee Pattison.

Ps. lxxxvi. 6. GIVE ear, O Lord, unto my prayer; and ponder the voice of my humble desires.
7. In the time of my trouble I will call upon thee: for thou hearest me.

Anthem 149.

T. Mee Pattison.

Ps. xcii. 1. IT is a good thing to give thanks unto the Lord, and to sing praises unto thy name, O thou most Highest:
2. To tell of thy lovingkindness early in the morning, and of thy truth in the night season.
3. Upon an instrument of ten strings, and upon the lute; upon a loud instrument, and upon the harp.
4. For thou, Lord, hast made me glad through thy works; and I will rejoice in giving praise for the operations of thy hands.

Anthem 150.

W. T. Best.

Ps. xcix. 2. THE Lord is great in Zion; and high above all people.
5. Magnify the Lord our God; for God is holy.
9. O magnify the Lord our God, and worship him upon his holy hill; for the Lord our God is holy. Amen.

Anthem 151.

Sir John Goss, Mus. D.

Ps. c. 1. O BE joyful in the Lord, all ye lands.
2. Serve the Lord with gladness; and come before his presence with a song.
3. Be ye sure that the Lord he is God: it is he that hath made us, and not we ourselves: we are his people, and the sheep of his pasture.
4. O go your way into his gates with thanksgiving, and into his courts with praise: be thankful unto him, and speak good of his name.
5. For the Lord is gracious; his mercy is everlasting; and his truth endureth from generation to generation.
Glory be to the Father, and to the Son, and to the Holy Ghost;
As it was in the beginning, is now, and ever shall be, world without end. Amen.

Anthem 152.

Sir George J. Elvey, Mus. D.

Ps. cv. 1. O GIVE thanks unto the Lord, and call upon his name: tell the people what things he hath done.
2. O let your songs be of him, and praise him: and let your talking be of all his wondrous works.
3. Rejoice in his holy name: let the heart of them rejoice that seek the Lord.

Anthem 153.

Sir John Goss, Mus. D.

Ps. cvi. 1. O GIVE thanks unto the Lord; for he is gracious: and his mercy endureth for ever.
2. Who can express the noble acts of the Lord, or shew forth all his praise?
Ps. cxviii. 22. The same stone which the builders refused is become the head stone in the corner.
23. This is the Lord's doing; and it is marvellous in our eyes.
29. O give thanks unto the Lord; for he is gracious: and his mercy endureth for ever.
Hallelujah. Amen.

Anthem 154.

Henry Smart.

Ps. cxviii. 14. THE Lord is my strength and my song, and is become my salvation.
17. I shall not die, but live, and declare the works of the Lord.
29. O give thanks unto the Lord; for he is gracious: and his mercy endureth for ever.

Anthem 155.

Sir George J. Elvey, Mus. D.

Ps. cxxii.   1. I WAS glad when they said unto me, We will go into the house of the Lord.
5. For there is the seat of judgment, even the seat of the house of David.
6. O pray for the peace of Jerusalem : they shall prosper that love thee.
7. Peace be within thy walls, and plenteousness within thy palaces.   Amen.

Anthem 156.

Sir George J. Elvey, Mus. D.

Ps. cxxviii.   1. BLESSED are they that fear the Lord, and walk in his ways.
2. O well is thee, and happy shalt thou be.

Anthem 157.

James Turle.

Ps. cxxxiv.   3. THE Lord that made heaven and earth give thee blessing out of Zion. Hallelujah. Amen.

Anthem 158.

Sir John Goss, Mus. D.

Ps. cxxxv.   1. O PRAISE the Lord. Laud ye the name of the Lord; praise it, O ye servants of the Lord.
2. Ye that stand in the house of the Lord, in the courts of the house of our God,
3. O praise the Lord ; for the Lord is gracious : O sing praises unto his name ; for it is lovely.
19. Praise the Lord, ye house of Israel : praise the Lord, ye house of Aaron.
20. Praise the Lord, ye house of Levi : ye that fear the Lord, praise the Lord.

Anthem 159.

George B. Allen, Mus. B.

Ps. cxxxvii.   1. BY the waters of Babylon we sat down and wept, when we remembered thee, O Zion.
2. As for our harps, we hanged them up upon the trees that are therein.
3. For they that led us away captive required of us then a song, and melody in our heaviness : Sing us one of the songs of Zion.
4. How shall we sing the Lord's song in a strange land ?
5. If I forget thee, O Jerusalem, let my right hand forget her cunning.
6. If I do not remember thee, let my tongue cleave to the roof of my mouth ; yea, if I prefer not Jerusalem in my mirth.
7. Remember the children of Edom, O Lord, in the day of Jerusalem ; how they said, Down with it, down with it, even to the ground.
8. O daughter of Babylon, wasted with misery; yea, happy shall he be that rewardeth thee as thou hast served us.
9. Blessed shall he be that dasheth thy children against the stones.

Anthem 160.

Rev. Sir F. A. Gore Ouseley, Bart., Mus. D.

Ps. cxli.   1. LORD, I call upon thee : haste thee unto me ; and consider my voice, when I cry unto thee.
2. Let my prayer be set forth in thy sight as the incense ; and let the lifting up of my hands be an evening sacrifice.

Anthem 161.

John E. West.

Ps. cxli.   1. LORD, I call upon thee : haste thee unto me ; and consider my voice, when I cry unto thee.
2. Let my prayer be set forth in thy sight as the incense ; and let the lifting up of my hands be an evening sacrifice. Amen.

Anthem 162.

Henry Baker, Mus. B.

Ps. cxli.   8. MINE eyes look unto thee, O Lord God : in thee is my trust ; O cast not out my soul.

Anthem 163.

Sir John Goss, Mus. D.

Ps. cxlv. 1. I WILL magnify thee, O God, my King; and I will praise thy name for ever and ever.
2. Every day will I give thanks unto thee; and praise thy name for ever and ever.
15. The eyes of all wait upon thee; and thou givest them their meat in due season.
16. Thou openest thine hand, and fillest all things living with plenteousness. Amen.

Anthem 164.

G. M. Garrett, M.A., Mus. D.

Ps. cxlv. 9. THE Lord is loving unto every man: and his mercy is over all his works.
10. All thy works praise thee, O God; and thy saints give thanks unto thee.
11. They show the glory of thy kingdom, and talk of thy power;
12. That thy power, thy glory, and the mightiness of thy kingdom might be known unto men.
13. Thy kingdom is an everlasting kingdom, and thy law is the truth. Amen.

Anthem 165.

Sir John Goss, Mus. D.

Ps. cxlvi. 1. PRAISE the Lord, O my soul.
2. While I live will I praise the Lord: yea, as long as I have any being, I will sing praises unto my God.
Ps. cxxii. 6. O pray for the peace of Jerusalem: they shall prosper that love thee.
7. Peace be within thy walls, and plenteousness within thy palaces.
8. For my brethren and companions' sakes, I will wish thee prosperity.
9. Yea, because of the house of the Lord our God, I will seek to do thee good.
Ps. cxxv. 1. They that put their trust in the Lord shall be even as the mount Zion, which may not be removed, but standeth fast for ever.
2. As the mountains are round about Jerusalem, so the Lord is round about his people from henceforth even for ever.

Anthem 166.

William Croft, Mus. D.

ISA. xii. 6. CRY aloud and shout, thou inhabitant of Zion: for great is the Holy One of Israel in the midst of thee.

Anthem 167.

Rev. Sir F. A. Gore Ouseley, Bart., Mus. D.

ISA. xxv. 1. O LORD, thou art my God; I will exalt thee, I will praise thy name; for thou hast done wonderful things; thy counsels of old are faithfulness and truth. Amen.

Anthem 168.

T. Tallis Trimnell, Mus. B.

ISA. xxvi. 3. THOU wilt keep him in perfect peace, whose mind is stayed on thee: because he trusteth in thee. Amen.

Anthem 169.

Sir John Stainer, M.A., Mus. D.

EZEK. xxxvi. 28. YE shall dwell in the land that I gave to your fathers; and ye shall be my people, and I will be your God.
30. I will multiply the fruit of the tree, and the increase of the field.
34. And the desolate land shall be tilled, whereas it lay desolate in the sight of all that passed by.
35. And they shall say, This land that was desolate is become like the garden of Eden.
Ps. cxxxvi. 1. Give thanks unto the Lord: his mercy endureth for ever.

O blessed is that land of God.
  Where saints abide for ever;
Where golden fields spread far and broad,
  Where flows the crystal river.
    O blessed, thrice blessed.

The strains of all its holy throng,
With ours to-day are blending;
Thrice blessed is that harvest song,
Which never hath an ending.
O blessed, thrice blessed. Amen.
W. Chatterton Dix.

Anthem 170.

Rev. Sir F. A. Gore Ouseley, Bart., Mus. D.

MAL. i. 11. FROM the rising of the sun unto the going down of the same my name shall be great among the Gentiles; and in every place incense shall be offered up unto my name: for my name shall be great among the Gentiles: thus saith the Lord!

Anthem 171.

Sir Arthur S. Sullivan, Mus. D.

TOBIT viii. 15. O GOD, thou art worthy to be praised with all pure and holy praise: therefore let the saints praise thee with all thy creatures; and let all thine angels and thine elect praise thee for ever.

16. Thou art to be praised, for thou hast made these thy servants joyful. Thou hast dealt with them according to thy great mercy.

17. Grant them mercy, O Lord, and finish their life in health with joy; for thou hast made these thy servants joyful.

Ps. xx. 2. The Lord send thee help from the sanctuary, and strengthen thee out of Zion;

4. Grant thee thy heart's desire, and fulfil all thy mind.

1. The Lord hear thee in the day of trouble; the name of the God of Jacob defend thee.

Anthem 172.

J. L. Hatton.

MATT. ii. 1. Now when Jesus was born in Bethlehem of Judæa in the days of Herod the king, behold, there came wise men from the east to Jerusalem,

2. Saying, Where is he that is born King of the Jews? for we have seen his star in the east, and have come to worship him.

LUKE i. 32. He shall be great, and shall be called the Son of the Highest: and the Lord God shall give unto him the throne of his father David:

33. And he shall reign over the house of Jacob for ever; and of his kingdom there shall be no end.

Hallelujah. Amen.

Anthem 173.

Henry Hiles, Mus. D.

MATT. v. 7. BLESSED are the merciful: for they shall obtain mercy.

3. Blessed are the poor in spirit: for their's is the kingdom of heaven.

8. Blessed are the pure in heart: for they shall see God.

Anthem 174.

A. L. Peace, Mus. D.

MATT. v. 10. BLESSED are they which are persecuted for righteousness' sake: for their's is the kingdom of heaven.

Anthem 175.

H. R. Couldrey.

MATT. xi. 28. COME unto me, all ye that labour and are heavy laden, and I will give you rest.

29. Take my yoke upon you, and learn of me; for I am meek and lowly in heart: and ye shall find rest unto your souls.

Anthems 176, 177, 178.

*176. A. L. Peace, Mus. D. 177. Sir George J. Elvey.
178. Sir John Stainer, M.A., Mus. D.*

LUKE i. 46. MY soul doth magnify the Lord,

47. And my spirit hath rejoiced in God my Saviour.

48. For he hath regarded the lowliness of his handmaiden: for, behold, from henceforth all generations shall call me blessed.

49. For he that is mighty hath magnified me ; and holy is his name.
50. And his mercy is on them that fear him throughout all generations.
51. He hath shewed strength with his arm ; he hath scattered the proud in the imagination of their hearts.
52. He hath put down the mighty from their seat, and hath exalted the humble and meek.
53. He hath filled the hungry with good things ; and the rich he hath sent empty away.
54. He, remembering his mercy, hath holpen his servant Israel ;
55. As he promised to our forefathers, Abraham and his seed, for ever.
Glory be to the Father, and to the Son, and to the Holy Ghost ;
As it was in the beginning, is now, and ever shall be, world without end. Amen.

Anthems 179, 180, 181.

*179. J. B. Dykes, Mus. D.   180. G. M. Garrett, Mus. D.
181. Sir John Stainer, M.A., Mus. D.*

LUKE i. 68. BLESSED be the Lord God of Israel ; for he hath visited and redeemed his people,
69. And hath raised up a mighty salvation for us in the house of his servant David ;
70. As he spake by the mouth of his holy prophets, which have been since the world began :
71. That we should be saved from our enemies, and from the hands of all that hate us ;
72. To perform the mercy promised to our forefathers, and to remember his holy covenant ;
73. To perform the oath which he sware to our forefather Abraham,
74. That he would give us, that we being delivered out of the hand of our enemies might serve him without fear,
75. In holiness and righteousness before him, all the days of our life.
76. And thou, child, shalt be called the prophet of the Highest : for thou shalt go before the face of the Lord to prepare his ways ;
77. To give knowledge of salvation unto his people for the remission of their sins,

78. Through the tender mercy of our God ; whereby the dayspring from on high hath visited us,
79. To give light to them that sit in darkness and in the shadow of death, and to guide our feet into the way of peace.
Glory be to the Father, and to the Son, and to the Holy Ghost ;
As it was in the beginning, is now, and ever shall be, world without end. Amen.

Anthem 182.

Sir John Goss, Mus. D.

LUKE ii. 10. BEHOLD, I bring you good tidings of great joy, which shall be to all people.
11. For unto you is born this day in the city of David a Saviour, which is Christ the Lord.

Anthem 183.

E. J. Hopkins, Mus. D.

LUKE ii. 15. LET us now go even unto Bethlehem, and see this thing which is come to pass, which the Lord hath made known unto us.
10. For the angel said unto us, Fear not : for, behold, I bring you good tidings of great joy, which shall be to all people.
11. For unto you is born this day in the city of David a Saviour, which is Christ the Lord.

Anthem 184.

Sir John Goss, Mus. D.

LUKE ii. 29. LORD, now lettest thou thy servant depart in peace, according to thy word :
30. For mine eyes have seen thy salvation,
31. Which thou hast prepared before the face of all people ;
32. To be a light to lighten the Gentiles, and to be the glory of thy people Israel.
Glory be to the Father, and to the Son, and to the Holy Ghost ;
As it was in the beginning, is now, and ever shall be, world without end. Amen.

Anthem 185.

Sir George J. Elvey, Mus. D.

LUKE xxiii. 28. DAUGHTERS of Jerusalem, weep not for me, but weep for yourselves, and for your children.

Anthem 186.

E. J. Hopkins, Mus. D.

LUKE xxiv. 5. WHY seek ye the living among the dead?

6. He is not here, but is risen: remember how he spake unto you when he was yet in Galilee,

7. Saying, The Son of man must be delivered into the hands of sinful men, and be crucified, and the third day rise again.

Anthem 187.

Sir John Goss, Mus. D.

JOHN iii. 16. GOD so loved the world, that he gave his only begotten Son, that whosoever believeth in him should not perish, but have everlasting life.

17. For God sent not his Son into the world to condemn the world; but that the world through him might be saved. Amen.

Anthem 188.

Sir W. Sterndale Bennett, Mus. D.

JOHN iv. 24. GOD is a Spirit: and they that worship him must worship him in spirit and in truth.

23. For the Father seeketh such to worship him.

Anthem 189.

Sir Robert P. Stewart, Mus. D.

JOHN xiv. 15. IF ye love me, keep my commandments.

16. And I will pray the Father, and he shall give you another Comforter;

17. Even the Spirit of truth; whom the world cannot receive, because it seeth him not, neither knoweth him: but ye know him; for he dwelleth with you, and shall be in you.

27. Peace I leave with you, my peace I give unto you. Let not your heart be troubled, neither let it be afraid.

Anthem 190.

Joseph Barnby.

ROM. xiii. 11. IT is high time to awake out of sleep: for now is our salvation nearer than when we believed.

12. The night is far spent, the day is at hand: let us therefore cast off the works of darkness, and let us put on the whole armour of light.

Anthem 191.

E. T. Chipp, Mus. D.

ROM. xiv. 11. As I live, saith the Lord, every knee shall bow to me, and every tongue shall confess to God.

12. So that every one shall give an account of himself to God.

ROM. ii. 6. Who will render to every man according to his deeds:

11. For there is no respect of persons with God.

ROM. viii. 14. For as many as are led by the Spirit of God, they are the sons of God.

ROM. xiv. 7. None of us liveth unto himself, and no man dieth to himself.

8. Whether we live, we live unto the Lord; and whether we die, we die unto the Lord: whether we live therefore, or die, we are the Lord's.

ROM. xi. 33. O the depth of the riches both of the wisdom and knowledge of God!

36. For of him, and through him, and to him, are all things: to whom be glory for ever. Amen.

Anthem 192.

Sir John Goss, Mus. D.

1 COR. v. 7. CHRIST our passover is sacrificed for us:

8. Therefore let us keep the feast, not with the old leaven, nor with the leaven of malice and wickedness; but with the unleavened bread of sincerity and truth.

Anthem 193.
Sir George J. Elvey, Mus. D.

1 COR. xv. 20. CHRIST is risen from the dead. Hallelujah.

ROM. vi. 10. In that he died, he died unto sin once: but in that he liveth, he liveth unto God. Hallelujah.

Anthem 194.
Sir John Goss, Mus. D.

1 THESS. iv. 14. IF we believe that Jesus died and rose again, even so them also which sleep in Jesus will God bring with him.

18. Wherefore comfort one another with these words.

Anthem 195.
S. S. Wesley, Mus. D.

1 PETER i. 3. BLESSED be the God and Father of our Lord Jesus Christ, which according to his abundant mercy hath begotten us again unto a lively hope by the resurrection of Jesus Christ from the dead,

4. To an inheritance incorruptible, and undefiled, that fadeth not away, reserved in heaven for you,

5. Who are kept by the power of God through faith unto salvation ready to be revealed at the last time.

15. But as he which hath called you is holy, so be ye holy in all manner of conversation.

17. Pass the time of your sojourning here in fear.

22. See that ye love one another with a pure heart fervently:

23. Being born again, not of corruptible seed, but of incorruptible, by the word of God.

24. For all flesh is as grass, and all the glory of man as the flower of grass. The grass withereth, and the flower thereof falleth away:

25. But the word of the Lord endureth for evermore. Amen.

Anthem 196.
William Boyce, Mus. D.

REV. vii. 12. BLESSING, and glory, and wisdom, and thanksgiving, and honour, and power, and might, be unto our God for ever and ever.

Hallelujah. Amen.

Anthem 197.
Sir John Stainer, M.A., Mus. D.

REV. vii. 13. HALLELUJAH. What are these that are arrayed in white robes? and whence came they?

14. These are they which came out of great tribulation, and have washed their robes, and made them white in the blood of the Lamb.

15. Hallelujah. Therefore are they before the throne of God, and serve him day and night in his temple.

16. They shall hunger no more, neither thirst any more; neither shall the sun light on them, nor any heat.

17. For the Lamb which is in the midst of the throne shall feed them, and shall lead them unto living fountains of waters: and God shall wipe away all tears from their eyes.

Anthem 198.
Spohr.

REV. xiv. 13. BLEST are the departed, who in the Lord are sleeping, from henceforth for evermore: they rest from their labours; and their works follow them.

Anthem 199.
Franz Abt.

O LORD most holy, O God most mighty, O loving Saviour, thee we would be praising with joyful lips; for thou hast redeemed us of thy grace and mercy.

WORDS OF ANTHEMS.

Teach us to know thee, teach us to love thee, make us to follow after holiness; so in temptation, and in the hour of sadness, we shall find comfort and help in thee.

Guide us, O loving Saviour; so in the hour of sadness we shall find comfort and help in thee. Amen.

Anthem 200.
Orlando Gibbons, Mus. D.

COLLECT. ALMIGHTY and everlasting God, mercifully look upon our infirmities; and in all our dangers and necessities stretch forth thy right hand to help and defend us, through Jesus Christ our Lord. Amen.

Anthem 201.
W. Hutchins Callcott.

LITURGY. GIVE peace in our time, O Lord; because there is none other that fighteth for us, but only thou, O God. Defend us, thy humble servants, in all assaults of our enemies.

Anthem 202.
Sir John Goss, Mus. D.

COLLECT. O SAVIOUR of the world, who by thy cross and precious blood hast redeemed us, save us, and help us, we humbly beseech thee, O Lord. Amen.

Anthem 203.
Sir John Goss, Mus. D.

COLLECT. ALMIGHTY and merciful God, of whose only gift it cometh that thy faithful people do unto thee true and laudable service; grant, we beseech thee, that we may so faithfully serve thee in this life, that we fail not finally to attain thy heavenly promises, through the merits of Jesus Christ our Lord. Amen.

Anthems 204, 205, 206.
204. J. B. Dykes, Mus. D. 205. A. L. Peace, Mus. D. 206. Henry Smart.

TE DEUM. 1. WE praise thee, O God: we acknowledge thee to be the Lord.

2. All the earth doth worship thee, the Father everlasting.
3. To thee all angels cry aloud: the heavens and all the powers therein.
4. To thee Cherubin and Seraphin continually do cry,
5. Holy, holy, holy, Lord God of Sabaoth;
6. Heaven and earth are full of the Majesty of thy glory.
7. The glorious company of the Apostles praise thee.
8. The goodly fellowship of the Prophets praise thee.
9. The noble army of Martyrs praise thee.
10. The holy Church throughout all the world doth acknowledge thee;
11. The Father of an infinite Majesty;
12. Thine honourable, true, and only Son;
13. Also the Holy Ghost, the Comforter.
14. Thou art the King of Glory, O Christ.
15. Thou art the everlasting Son of the Father.
16. When thou tookest upon thee to deliver man, thou didst not abhor the Virgin's womb.
17. When thou hadst overcome the sharpness of death, thou didst open the kingdom of heaven to all believers.
18. Thou sittest at the right hand of God, in the glory of the Father.
19. We believe that thou shalt come to be our Judge.
20. We therefore pray thee, help thy servants whom thou hast redeemed with thy precious blood.
21. Make them to be numbered with thy saints in glory everlasting.
22. O Lord, save thy people, and bless thine heritage.
23. Govern them, and lift them up for ever.
24. Day by day we magnify thee;
25. And we worship thy Name ever world without end.
26. Vouchsafe, O Lord, to keep us this day without sin.
27. O Lord, have mercy upon us, have mercy upon us.
28. O Lord, let thy mercy lighten upon us, as our trust is in thee.
29. O Lord, in thee have I trusted; let me never be confounded.

Anthem 207.

E. J. Hopkins, Mus. D.

THE APOSTLES' CREED. I BELIEVE in God the Father Almighty, Maker of heaven and earth :

And in Jesus Christ his only Son, our Lord ; who was conceived by the Holy Ghost, born of the Virgin Mary, suffered under Pontius Pilate, was crucified, dead, and buried ; he descended into hell ; the third day he rose again from the dead ; he ascended into heaven, and sitteth on the right hand of God the Father Almighty ; from thence he shall come to judge the quick and the dead.

I believe in the Holy Ghost ; the holy catholic Church ; the communion of saints ; the forgiveness of sins ; the resurrection of the body ; and the life everlasting. Amen.

Anthem 208.

Sir John Goss, Mus. D.

THE NICENE CREED. I BELIEVE in one God, the Father Almighty, Maker of heaven and earth, and of all things visible and invisible :

And in one Lord Jesus Christ, the only-begotten Son of God, begotten of his Father before all worlds, God of God, Light of Light, very God of very God, begotten, not made, being of one substance with the Father, by whom all things were made : who for us men, and for our salvation, came down from heaven, and was incarnate by the Holy Ghost of the Virgin Mary, and was made man, and was crucified also for us under Pontius Pilate : he suffered and was buried, and the third day he rose again according to the Scriptures, and ascended into heaven, and sitteth on the right hand of the Father : and he shall come again with glory to judge both the quick and the dead ; whose kingdom shall have no end.

And I believe in the Holy Ghost, the Lord and Giver of life ; who proceedeth from the Father and the Son ; who with the Father and the Son together is worshipped and glorified, who spake by the prophets. And I believe one catholic and apostolic Church ; I acknowledge one baptism for the remission of sins ; and I look for the resurrection of the dead, and the life of the world to come. Amen.

Anthem 209.

Novello.

Ps. cxxxvii. 1 4.

Solo. To thee, great Lord o'er all
   In earth and sea and sky,
   Thy people humbly fall,
   With mournful plaint they cry
Chorus. O hear us from thy throne ;
   Descend and save thine own.

Solo. Where Babylon's waters flow
   In sadd'ning streams along,
   They sat them down in woe,
   And, weeping, made their song :
Chorus. O'er Zion's waste we mourn,
   Oh, when shall we return ?

Solo. Their foes, with impious taunt,
   Required a song of praise,
   Whilst far from youthful haunt,
   Our home, and happier days :
Chorus. Ah, no ! our harps are hung
   On willow's bough, unstrung.

Chorus. To thee, great Lord o'er all
   In earth and sea and sky,
   Thy people humbly fall,
   With pressing suit we cry :
   O hear us from thy throne,
   Descend and save thine own.

Anthem 210.

W. T. Best.

LUKE ii. 8-15.

WHILE shepherds watched their flocks by night,
   All seated on the ground,
The angel of the Lord came down,
   And glory shone around.
Fear not, said he, for mighty dread
   Had seized their troubled mind ;
Glad tidings of great joy I bring
   To you, and all mankind.

To you, in David's town, this day
   Is born, of David's line,
The Saviour, who is Christ the Lord ;
   And this shall be the sign :

The heavenly Babe you there shall find
   To human view displayed,
All meanly wrapped in swathing bands,
   And in a manger laid.

Thus spake the seraph : and forthwith
   Appeared a shining throng
Of angels, praising God ; who thus
   Addressed their joyful song :
All glory be to God on high,
   And on the earth be peace ;
Goodwill henceforth from Heaven to men,
   Begin and never cease.   Amen.

Anthems 211, 212.

211. Thomas Attwood.   212. Sir George J. Elvey, Mus. D.

COME, Holy Ghost, our souls inspire,
And lighten with celestial fire ;
Thou the anointing Spirit art,
Who dost thy sevenfold gifts impart.
Thy blessed unction from above
Is comfort, life, and fire of love.

Enable with perpetual light
The dulness of our blinded sight ;
Anoint and cheer our soilèd face
With the abundance of thy grace :
Keep far our foes, give peace at home ;
Where thou art Guide no ill can come.

Teach us to know the Father, Son,
And Thee of Both, to be but One ;
That, through the ages all along,
This may be our endless song :
   Praise to thy eternal merit,
   Father, Son, and Holy Spirit.

Anthem 213.

Rev. H. H. Woodward, M.A., Mus. B.

THE radiant morn hath passed away,
And spent too soon her golden store ;
The shadows of departing day
   Creep on once more.

Our life is but a fading dawn,
Its glorious noon how quickly past ;
Lead us, O Christ, when all is gone,
   Safe home at last—

Where saints are clothed in spotless white,
And evening shadows never fall ;
Where thou, Eternal Light of Light,
   Art Lord of all.

Anthem 214.

Charles Gounod.

FROM thy love as a Father,
   O Lord, teach us to gather
   That Life will conquer Death :
They who seek things eternal
Shall rise to light supernal
   On wings of lowly faith.

Anthem 215.

Sir George A. Macfarren, Mus. D.

O HOLY GHOST, into our minds
Send down thy heavenly light ;
Kindle our hearts with fervent zeal,
To serve God day and night.

Thou art the very Comforter,
In grief and all distress ;
The heavenly gift of God most high,
No tongue can it express.

Such measures of thy powerful grace
Grant to us, Lord, we pray,
That thou may'st be our Comforter
At the last awful day.   Amen.

Anthem 216.

Mendelssohn.

GRANT us thy peace, Almighty Lord,
Thou source of every blessing !
Feeble and frail, trust we thy word,
All things in thee possessing—
In thee is our hope and safety.

Index of Words of Anthems.*

GIVING THEIR COMPOSERS, PUBLISHERS, AND SOURCES.

FIRST LINE.	COMPOSER.	PUBLISHER AND SOURCE.	NO.
Almighty and everlasting God	Orlando Gibbons, Mus. D.	Novello's Musical Times, 129	209
Almighty and merciful God	Sir John Goss, Mus. D.	Novello's Musical Times, 500	205
As I live, saith the Lord	E. T. Chipp, Mus. D.	Novello's 8vo Anthems, 311	191
As pants the hart for cooling streams	Spohr. Arr. by James Stimpson	Novello's Musical Times, 175	123
Awake up, my glory	A. L. Peace, Mus. D.	Novello, Ewer, and Co.	140
Behold, I bring you good tidings	Sir John Goss, Mus. D.	Novello's Musical Times, 178	182
Blessed are the merciful	Henry Hiles, Mus. D.	Novello's Musical Times, 312	173
Blessed are they that fear the Lord	Sir George J. Elvey, Mus. D.	Novello's Musical Times, 516	156
Blessed are they which are persecuted	A. L. Peace, Mus. D.	Novello, Ewer, and Co.	174
Blessed be the God and Father	S. S. Wesley, Mus. D.	Novello's 8vo Anthems, 15	195
Blessed be the Lord God of Israel	Rev. J. B. Dykes, Mus. D.	No. 2 of Morning and Evening Service in F. Novello, Ewer, and Co.	179
Blessed be the Lord God of Israel	G. M. Garrett, M.A., Mus. D.	No. 2 of Morning and Evening Service No. 1 in D. Novello, Ewer, and Co.	180
Blessed be the Lord God of Israel	Sir John Stainer, M.A., Mus. D.	No. 2 of Morning and Evening Service No. 3 in B♭. Novello, Ewer, and Co.	181
Blessing, and glory, and wisdom	William Boyce, Mus. D.	Novello's Musical Times, 259	196
Blest are the departed	Spohr.	Novello's Musical Times, 161	198
Bow thine ear, O Lord, and hear	William Bird	Novello's 8vo Anthems, 118	147
By the waters of Babylon	George B. Allen, Mus. B.	Novello's Musical Times, 198	159
Call to remembrance thy tender mercies	Vincent Novello	Novello's Musical Times, 336	149
Christ is risen from the dead	Sir George J. Elvey, Mus. D.	Novello's Musical Times, 229	193
Christ our passover is sacrificed for us	Sir John Goss, Mus. D.	Novello's Musical Times, 163	192
Come, Holy Ghost, our souls inspire	Thomas Attwood.	Novello's Musical Times, 170	211
Come, Holy Ghost, our souls inspire	Sir George J. Elvey, Mus. D.	Novello's 8vo Anthems, 281	212
Come unto me, all ye that labour	H. R. Couldrey	Novello's 8vo Anthems, 256	175
Cry aloud and shout	William Croft, Mus. D.	Novello's Musical Times, 61	166
Daughters of Jerusalem	Sir George J. Elvey, Mus. D.	Novello's Musical Times, 290	185
From the rising of the sun	Sir F. A. Gore Ouseley, Bart., Mus. D.	Novello's Musical Times, 570	170
From thy love as a Father	Charles Gounod	Novello's Musical Times, 519	214
Give ear, O Lord, unto my prayer	T. Mee Pattison	Novello's 8vo Anthems, 227	148
Give peace in our time, O Lord	W. Hutchins Callcott.	Novello's Musical Times, 503	201
God is a Spirit	Sir W. Sterndale Bennett, Mus. D.	Novello, Ewer, and Co.	188
God is our hope and strength	Maurice Greene, Mus. D.	Novello's 8vo Anthems, 131	135
God so loved the world	Sir John Goss, Mus. D.	Novello's Musical Times, 599	157
Grant us thy peace, Almighty Lord	Mendelssohn	Novello's Musical Times, 432	216
Hallelujah! What are these?	Sir John Stainer, M.A., Mus. D.	Novello's 8vo Anthems, 197	197
Hear my prayer, O God, incline	Mendelssohn	Novello's 8vo Anthems, 339	139
Hear, O Lord, and have mercy upon me	Sir F. A. Gore Ouseley, Bart., Mus. D.	Novello's 8vo Anthems, 162	150
Hear, O thou shepherd of Israel	J. Clarke-Whitfeld, Mus. D.	Novello's 8vo Anthems, 203	144
How goodly are thy tents, O Jacob	Sir F. A. Gore Ouseley, Bart., Mus. D.	Novello's Musical Times, 247	141
I believe in God the Father Almighty	E. J. Hopkins, Mus. D.	The Apostles' Creed in monotone. Weekes and Co.	207
I believe in one God, the Father Almighty	Sir John Goss, Mus. D.	The Nicene Creed for voices in unison. Novello, Ewer, and Co.	208
If we believe that Jesus died	Sir John Goss, Mus. D.	Novello's Musical Times, 448	194
If ye love me, keep my commandments	Sir Robert P. Stewart, Mus. D.	Novello's Musical Times, 505	189
In Jewry is God known	J. Clarke-Whitfeld, Mus. D.	Novello's Musical Times, 98	142
In the Lord put I my trust	Sir Robert P. Stewart, Mus. D.	Novello's 8vo Anthems, 282	125
It is a good thing to give thanks	T. Mee Pattison	Novello's 8vo Anthems, 231	149
It is high time to awake out of sleep	Joseph Barnby	Novello's Musical Times, 321	190
I waited for the Lord	Mendelssohn.	Novello's 8vo Choruses, 169a	133
I was glad when they said unto me	Sir George J. Elvey, Mus. D.	Novello's 8vo Anthems, 52	155
I will cry unto God with my voice	Charles Steggall, Mus. D.	Novello's 8vo Anthems, 73	143
I will lay me down in peace	Henry Gadsby	Novello's 8vo Anthems, 195	123

* Music to be had from the Publishers of the several Anthems.

INDEX OF WORDS OF ANTHEMS.

FIRST LINE.	COMPOSER.	PUBLISHER AND SOURCE.	NO.
I will lay me down in peace	A. C. Mackenzie, Mus. D.	Novello's Musical Times, 451	124
I will magnify thee, O God, my King	Sir John Goss, Mus. D.	Novello's 8vo Anthems, 27	163
Keep innocency, and take heed	J. Baptiste Calkin	Morley's Original Anthems, 11	131
Let us now go even unto Bethlehem	E. J. Hopkins, Mus. D.	Novello's Musical Times, 114	183
Lift up your heads, O ye gates	J. L. Hopkins, Mus. D.	Novello's 8vo Anthems, 18	128
Lord, how long wilt thou forget me?	Mendelssohn	Novello's Musical Times, 376	126
Lord, I call upon thee	Sir F. A. Gore Ouseley, Bart., Mus. D.	Novello's Musical Times, 401	160
Lord, I call upon thee	John E. West	Novello's Musical Times, 492	161
Lord, now lettest thou thy servant	Sir John Goss, Mus. D.	Magnificat and Nunc Dimittis in A. Novello, Ewer, and Co.	184
Lord, who shall dwell in thy tabernacle?	J. Varley Roberts, Mus. D.	Novello's 8vo Anthems, 207	127
Mine eyes look unto thee, O Lord God	Henry Baker, Mus. B.	Novello's 8vo Anthems, 211	162
My soul doth magnify the Lord	A. L. Peace, Mus. D.	Magnificat and Nunc Dimittis in D. Service No. 2. Novello, Ewer, and Co.	176
My soul doth magnify the Lord	Sir George J. Elvey, Mus. D.	Magnificat and Nunc Dimittis in E. Novello, Ewer, and Co.	177
My soul doth magnify the Lord	Sir John Stainer, M.A., Mus. D.	Magnificat and Nunc Dimittis in D in Chant form. No. 2. Novello	178
Now when Jesus was born in Bethlehem	J. L. Hatton	Metzler's Choir, 410	172
O be joyful in the Lord, all ye lands	Sir John Goss, Mus. D.	Te Deum and Jubilate in A. Novello	151
O clap your hands together	T. Tallis Trimnell, Mus. B.	Novello's 8vo Anthems, 217	136
O give thanks unto the Lord, and call	Sir George J. Elvey, Mus. D.	Novello's 8vo Anthems, 16	152
O give thanks unto the Lord; for he	Sir John Goss, Mus. D.	Novello's 8vo Anthems, 42	153
O God, thou art worthy to be praised	Sir Arthur S. Sullivan, Mus. D.	Novello's 8vo Anthems, 34	171
O Holy Ghost, into our minds	Sir George A. Macfarren, Mus. D.	Novello's Musical Times, 266	215
O how amiable are thy dwellings	Joseph Barnby	Novello's 8vo Anthems, 47	145
O how amiable are thy dwellings	T. Mee Pattison	Novello's 8vo Anthems, 233	146
O Lord most holy, O God most mighty	Franz Abt	Novello's Musical Times, 386	199
O Lord my God, hear thou the prayer	S. S. Wesley, Mus. D.	Novello's Musical Times, 314	122
O Lord, thou art my God	Sir F. A. Gore Ouseley, Bart., Mus. D.	Novello's Musical Times, 306	167
O praise the Lord. Laud ye the name	Sir John Goss, Mus. D.	Novello's Musical Times, 168	153
O Saviour of the world	Sir John Goss, Mus. D.	Novello's Musical Times, 408	202
Praise the Lord, O my soul	Sir John Goss, Mus. D.	Novello's 8vo Anthems, 21	165
Save me, O God, for thy name's sake	J. L. Hopkins, Mus. D.	Novello's 8vo Anthems, 257	133
Send out thy light and thy truth	Charles Gounod	Metzler and Co.	134
The Lord is great in Zion	W. T. Best	Novello's 8vo Anthems, 44	150
The Lord is loving unto every man	G. M. Garrett, M.A., Mus. D.	Novello's 8vo Anthems, 39	164
The Lord is my strength and my song	Henry Smart	Novello's Musical Times, 398	154
The Lord that made heaven and earth	James Turle	Novello's 8vo Anthems, 84	157
The radiant morn hath passed away	Rev. H. H. Woodward, M.A., Mus. B.	Novello's Musical Times, 472	213
The sacrifices of God are a broken spirit	J. Baptiste Calkin	Novello's Musical Times, 464	137
Thou visitest the earth, and blessed it	W. Hutchins Callcott	Novello's 8vo Anthems, 191	141
Thou wilt keep him in perfect peace	T. Tallis Trimnell, Mus. B.	Novello's Musical Times, 522	168
To thee, great Lord o'er all	Rossini	Novello's Musical Times, 123	209
We praise thee, O God	Rev. J. B. Dykes, Mus. D.	Novello's Parish Choir Book, 26	204
We praise thee, O God	A. L. Peace, Mus. D.	Te Deum Laudamus and Benedictus in D. Service No. 2. Novello	205
We praise thee, O God	Henry Smart	Novello's Parish Choir Book, 32	206
What are these that are arrayed?	Sir John Stainer, M.A., Mus. D.	Novello's 8vo Anthems, 57	197
While shepherds watched their flocks	W. T. Best	Novello's Musical Times, 442	210
Why seek ye the living among the dead?	E. J. Hopkins, Mus. D.	Novello's Musical Times, 181	186
Ye shall dwell in the land that I gave	Sir John Stainer, M.A., Mus. D.	Novello's Musical Times, 414	169